Microsoft

MOS Study Guide for Microsoft Access Expert Exam MO-500

Paul McFedries

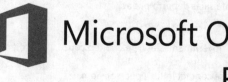
Microsoft Office Specialist
Exam MO-500

MOS Study Guide for Microsoft Access Expert Exam MO-500

ISBN-13: 978-0-13-662832-3
ISBN-10: 0-13-662832-X

Library of Congress Control Number: 2020933014

1 2020

Trademarks

Warning and Disclaimer

Special Sales

For information about buying this title in bulk quantities, or for special sales opportunities (which may include electronic versions; custom cover designs; and content particular to your business, training goals, marketing focus, or branding interests), please contact our corporate sales department at corpsales@pearsoned.com or (800) 382-3419.

For government sales inquiries, please contact governmentsales@pearsoned.com.

For questions about sales outside the U.S., please contact intlcs@pearson.com.

Editor-in-Chief
Brett Bartow

Executive Editor
Loretta Yates

Development Editor
Songlin Qiu

Managing Editor
Sandra Schroeder

Senior Project Editor
Tracey Croom

Sponsoring Editor
Charvi Arora

Copy Editor
Elizabeth Welch

Indexer
Cheryl Ann Lenser

Proofreader
Abigail Manheim

Technical Editor
Boyd Nolan

Editorial Assistant
Cindy Teeters

Cover Designer
Twist Creative, Seattle

Compositor
codeMantra

Contents

3   Create and modify queries   85

Introduction

The Microsoft Office Specialist (MOS) certification program has been designed to validate your knowledge of and ability to use programs in the Microsoft Office 365 and Microsoft Office 2019 suite of programs. This book has been designed to guide you in studying the types of tasks you are likely to be required to demonstrate in Exam MO-500, "Microsoft Access Expert (Access and Access 2019)."

Who this book is for

MOS Study Guide for Microsoft Access Expert Exam MO-500 is designed for experienced computer users seeking Microsoft Office Specialist certification in Access 365 and Access 2019.

MOS exams for individual programs are practical rather than theoretical. You must demonstrate that you can complete certain tasks or projects rather than simply answer questions about program features. The successful MOS certification candidate will have at least six months of experience using all aspects of the program on a regular basis—for example, using Access at work or school to create and manage databases, build database tables, import and export data, design and run queries, create and format forms, and design detail and summary reports.

As a certification candidate, you probably have a lot of experience with the program you want to become certified in. Many of the procedures described in this book will be familiar to you; others might not be. Read through each study section and ensure that you are familiar with the procedures, concepts, and tools discussed. In some cases, images depict the tools you will use to perform procedures related to the skill set. Study the images and ensure that you are familiar with the options available for each tool.

How this book is organized

The exam coverage is divided into chapters representing broad skill sets that correlate to the functional groups covered by the exam. Each chapter is divided into sections addressing groups of related skills that correlate to the exam objectives. Each section includes review information, generic procedures, and practice tasks you can complete on your own while studying. We provide practice files you can use to work through the practice tasks and result files you can use to check your work. You can practice the generic procedures in this book by using the practice files supplied or by using your own files.

Throughout this book, you will find Exam Strategy tips that present information about the scope of study that is necessary to ensure that you achieve mastery of a skill set and are successful in your certification effort.

Download the practice files

Before you can complete the practice tasks in this book, you need to copy the book's practice files and result files to your computer. Download the compressed (zipped) folder from the following page, and extract the files from it to a folder (such as your Documents folder) on your computer:

MicrosoftPressStore.com/MOSAccessExpert500/downloads

IMPORTANT The Access 365 and Access 2019 programs are not available from this website. You should purchase and install one of those programs before using this book.

You will save the completed versions of practice files that you modify while working through the practice tasks in this book. If you later want to repeat the practice tasks, you can download the original practice files again.

The following table lists the practice files provided for this book.

Folder and objective group	Practice files	Result files
MOSAccessExpert2019\Objective1 Manage databases	AccessExpert_1-1.accdb AccessExpert_1-2.accdb AccessExpert_1-3.accdb	AccessExpert_1-1_ results.accdb AccessExpert_1-2_ results.accdb AccessExpert_1-3_ results.accdb

Folder and objective group	Practice files	Result files
MOSAccessExpert2019\Objective2 Create and modify tables	AccessExpert_2-1.accdb AccessExpert_2-1.csv AccessExpert_2-1.html AccessExpert_2-1.txt AccessExpert_2-1.xlsx AccessExpert_2-1.xml AccessExpert_2-1.xsd AccessExpert_2-2.accdb AccessExpert_2-3.accdb AccessExpert_2-4.accdb	AccessExpert_2-1_results.accdb AccessExpert_2-2_results.accdb AccessExpert_2-3_results.accdb AccessExpert_2-4_results.accdb
MOSAccessExpert2019\Objective3 Create and modify queries	AccessExpert_3-1.accdb AccessExpert_3-2.accdb	AccessExpert_3-1_results.accdb AccessExpert_3-2_results.accdb
MOSAccessExpert2019\Objective4 Modify forms in Layout view	AccessExpert_4-1.accdb AccessExpert_4-2.accdb AccessExpert_4-2.jpg	AccessExpert_4-1_results.accdb AccessExpert_4-2_results.accdb
MOSAccessExpert2019\Objective5 Modify reports in Layout view	AccessExpert_5-1.accdb AccessExpert_5-2.accdb	AccessExpert_5-1_results.accdb AccessExpert_5-2_results.accdb

Adapt procedure steps

This book contains many images of user interface elements that you'll work with while performing tasks in Access on a Windows computer. Depending on your screen resolution or program window width, the Access ribbon on your screen might look different from that shown in this book. (If you turn on Touch mode, the ribbon displays significantly fewer commands than in Mouse mode.) As a result, procedural instructions that involve the ribbon might require a little adaptation.

Simple procedural instructions use this format:

→ On the **Home** tab, in the **Sort & Filter** group, click the **Filter** button.

If the command is in a list, our instructions use this format:

→ On the **Home** tab, in the **Sort & Filter** group, click **Advanced Filter Options**, and then, in the **Advanced Filter Options** list, click **Filter By Form**.

If differences between your display settings and ours cause a button to appear differently on your screen from how it does in this book, you can easily adapt the steps to locate the command. First click the specified tab, then locate the specified group. If a group has been collapsed into a group list or under a group button, click the list or button to display the group's commands. If you can't immediately identify the button you want, point to likely candidates to display their names in ScreenTips.

The instructions in this book assume that you're interacting with on-screen elements on your computer by clicking (with a mouse, touchpad, or other hardware device). If you're using a different method—for example, if your computer has a touchscreen interface and you're tapping the screen (with your finger or a stylus)—substitute the applicable tapping action when you interact with a user interface element.

Instructions in this book refer to user interface elements that you click or tap on the screen as buttons and to physical buttons that you press on a keyboard as keys, to conform to the standard terminology used in documentation for these products.

Ebook edition

If you're reading the ebook edition of this book, you can do the following:

- Search the full text
- Print
- Copy and paste

You can purchase and download the ebook edition from the Microsoft Press Store at:

MicrosoftPressStore.com/MOSAccessExpert500/detail

Errata, updates, & book support

We've made every effort to ensure the accuracy of this book and its companion content. If you discover an error, please submit it to us through the link at:

MicrosoftPressStore.com/MOSAccessExpert500/errata

For additional book support and information, please visit:

www.MicrosoftPressStore.com/Support

For help with Microsoft software and hardware, go to:

https://support.microsoft.com

Stay in touch

Let's keep the conversation going! We're on Twitter at:

https://twitter.com/MicrosoftPress

Taking a Microsoft Office Specialist exam

Desktop computing proficiency is increasingly important in today's business world. When screening, hiring, and training employees, employers can feel reassured by relying on the objectivity and consistency of technology certification to ensure the competence of their workforce. As an employee or job seeker, you can use technology certification to prove that you already have the skills you need to succeed, saving current and future employers the time and expense of training you.

Microsoft Office Specialist certification

Microsoft Office Specialist certification is designed to assist students and information workers in validating their skills with Office programs. The following certification paths are available:

- A Microsoft Office Specialist (MOS) is an individual who has demonstrated proficiency by passing a certification exam in one or more Office programs, including Microsoft Word, Excel, PowerPoint, Outlook, or Access.

- A Microsoft Office Specialist Expert (MOS Expert) is an individual who has taken his or her knowledge of Office to the next level and has demonstrated by passing Core and Expert certification exams that he or she has mastered the more advanced features of Word or Excel.

- A Microsoft Office Specialist Master (MOS Master) is an individual who has demonstrated a broader knowledge of Office skills by passing the Word Core and Expert exams, the Excel Core and Expert exams, the PowerPoint exam, and the Access or Outlook exam.

Selecting a certification path

When deciding which certifications you would like to pursue, assess the following:

- The program and program version(s) with which you are familiar
- The length of time you have used the program and how frequently you use it
- Whether you have had formal or informal training in the use of that program
- Whether you use most or all of the available program features
- Whether you are considered a go-to resource by business associates, friends, and family members who have difficulty with the program

Candidates for MOS certification are expected to successfully complete a wide range of standard business tasks. Successful candidates generally have six or more months of experience with the specific Office program, including either formal, instructor-led training or self-study using MOS-approved books, guides, or interactive computer-based materials.

Candidates for MOS Expert and MOS Master certification are expected to successfully complete more complex tasks that involve using the advanced functionality of the program. Successful candidates generally have at least six months, and might have several years, of experience with the programs, including formal, instructor-led training or self-study using MOS-approved materials.

Test-taking tips

Every MOS certification exam is developed from a set of exam skill standards (referred to as the *objective domain*) that are derived from studies of how the Office programs are used in the workplace. Because these skill standards dictate the scope of each exam, they provide critical information about how to prepare for certification. This book follows the structure of the published exam objectives.

See Also For more information about the book structure, see "How this book is organized" in the introduction.

The MOS certification exams are performance based and require you to complete business-related tasks in the program for which you are seeking certification. For example, you might be presented with a document and told to insert and format additional document elements. Your score on the exam reflects how many of the requested tasks you complete within the allotted time.

Here is some helpful information about taking the exam:

- Keep track of the time. Your exam time does not officially begin until after you finish reading the instructions provided at the beginning of the exam. During the exam, the amount of time remaining is shown in the exam instruction window. You can't pause the exam after you start it.

- Pace yourself. At the beginning of the exam, you will receive information about the tasks that are included in the exam. During the exam, the number of completed and remaining tasks is shown in the exam instruction window.

- Read the exam instructions carefully before beginning. Follow all the instructions provided completely and accurately.

- If you have difficulty performing a task, you can restart it without affecting the result of any completed tasks, or you can skip the task and come back to it after you finish the other tasks on the exam.

- Enter requested information as it appears in the instructions, but without duplicating the formatting unless you are specifically instructed to do so. For example, the text and values you are asked to enter might appear in the instructions in bold and underlined text, but you should enter the information without applying these formats.

- Close all dialog boxes before proceeding to the next exam item unless you are specifically instructed not to do so.

- Don't close task panes before proceeding to the next exam item unless you are specifically instructed to do so.

- If you are asked to print a document, worksheet, chart, report, or slide, perform the task, but be aware that nothing will actually be printed.

- Don't worry about extra keystrokes or mouse clicks. Your work is scored based on its result, not on the method you use to achieve that result (unless a specific method is indicated in the instructions).

- If a computer problem occurs during the exam (for example, if the exam does not respond or the mouse no longer functions) or if a power outage occurs, contact a testing center administrator immediately. The administrator will restart the computer and return the exam to the point where the interruption occurred, with your score intact.

Exam Strategy This book includes special tips for effectively studying for the Microsoft Office Specialist exams in Exam Strategy paragraphs such as this one.

Certification benefits

At the conclusion of the exam, you will receive a score report, indicating whether you passed the exam. If your score meets or exceeds the passing standard (the minimum required score), you will be contacted by email by the Microsoft Certification Program team. The email message you receive will include your Microsoft Certification ID and links to online resources, including the Microsoft Certified Professional site. On this site, you can download or order a printed certificate, create a virtual business card, order an ID card, review and share your certification transcript, access the Logo Builder, and access other useful and interesting resources, including special offers from Microsoft and affiliated companies.

Depending on the level of certification you achieve, you will qualify to display one of three logos on your business card and other personal promotional materials. These logos attest to the fact that you are proficient in the applications or cross-application skills necessary to achieve the certification. Using the Logo Builder, you can create a personalized certification logo that includes the MOS logo and the specific programs in which you have achieved certification. If you achieve MOS certification in multiple programs, you can include multiple certifications in one logo.

For more information

To learn more about the Microsoft Office Specialist exams and related courseware, visit:

www.certiport.com/mos

About the Author

Paul McFedries is a Microsoft Access and database expert and full-time technical writer. Paul has been authoring computer books since 1991 and has nearly 100 books to his credit, which combined have sold more than 4 million copies worldwide. His titles include the Microsoft Press Publishing book *Formulas and Functions for Microsoft Excel 2019*, the Que Publishing books *My Office 2016*, *My Office for iPad*, *Windows 10 In Depth* (with coauthor Brian Knittel), and *PCs for Grownups*, as well as the Wiley Publishing books *Teach Yourself VISUALLY Microsoft Access* and *Excel Data Analysis*. Please drop by Paul's personal website at www.mcfedries.com or follow Paul on Twitter at twitter.com/paulmcf.

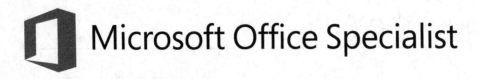

Microsoft Office Specialist

Exam MO-500

Microsoft Access Expert (Access and Access 2019)

This book covers the skills you need to have for certification as a Microsoft Office Expert in Access 365 and Access 2019. Specifically, you need to be able to complete tasks that demonstrate the following skills:

1   Manage databases
2   Create and modify tables
3   Create and modify queries
4   Modify forms in Layout view
5   Modify reports in Layout view

With these skills, you can populate and manage the types of databases most commonly used in a business environment.

Prerequisites

We assume that you have been working with Access 2019 for at least six months and that you know how to carry out fundamental tasks that are not specifically mentioned in the objectives for this Microsoft Office Specialist exam.

The certification exam and the content of this book address the processes of managing and modifying Access databases. We assume that you are familiar with the Microsoft Office ribbon and that you understand basic Access features—for example, that you know how to create databases and enter and edit data. We also assume you are familiar with the definition and function of relational databases and database objects such as tables and forms. To provide context and an opportunity for review, the following list provides brief explanations of five important terms:

- **Table** Defines the data stored in a database. Tables are composed of fields, and each field is defined as a specific data type (text, number, date, or another data type). Each field also has certain properties. For example, you can specify that a field is required. You can also define the size of a field (such as the maximum number of characters a field can contain). Users of a database fill in fields (and must fill in required fields) with values to create a record in the database. In most tables, each record is identified by a unique value called a *primary key*, which might be a single field (such as a product ID) or a combination of fields.

- **Relationship** Helps maintain the integrity of the information in a database and reduce data redundancy. You can create several types of relationships between tables in an Access database. In a one-to-many relationship, a record in one table can be related to one or many records in another. You can also create one-to-one relationships and many-to-many relationships. Relationships are created by linking a table's foreign key (such as a customer ID field in an order table) with another table's primary key (the customer ID field in the customer table). Relationships protect data integrity by preventing you from creating orphan records (for example, an order with no customer). Relationships help reduce data redundancy by letting you store information in separate tables that you link together. For example, you can create a customer table and then relate each order in an order table to the record for a specific customer. This prevents you from having to enter a custom record for each separate order.

- **Query** Can be used to select records that meet specific criteria and to perform actions such as updating a group of records. To build a select query, you add fields from one or more tables and then define criteria that Access uses to retrieve the records you want to view. For example, you might want to retrieve records with a certain value in a date field (all records created after 1/1/2020, for example) or records associated with a specific project. Using criteria, you can also create and run action queries that insert, update, or delete selected records.

- **Form** Used to display, enter, and edit data. Forms are often bound to tables (or to queries) that serve as the form's record source. Forms use controls such as text boxes, check boxes, and list boxes to provide a user interface for a database. Forms can also be used to confirm and execute database operations and to navigate from one database object to another. Access provides several built-in form designs, a gallery of form controls, and tools you use to design and lay out a form.

- **Report** Used to share and present data and to summarize data for a specific field or fields. You might print reports for a meeting or distribute them electronically as PDF files or in email.

Objective group 1

Manage databases

The skills tested in this section of the Microsoft Office Specialist Expert exam for Microsoft Access 365 and Microsoft Access 2019 relate to managing database structure, relationships, printing, and exporting. Specifically, the following objectives are associated with this set of skills:

1.1 Modify database structure

1.2 Manage table relationships and keys

1.3 Print and export data

Every Access database exists within a larger ecosystem of objects, including tables, queries, forms, and reports. Mastering database management requires knowing not only how to import data into Access, but also how to work with and create sophisticated relationships between objects.

This chapter guides you in studying methods for importing data, deleting database objects, working with objects in the Navigation Pane, understanding table relationships, setting primary and foreign keys, enforcing referential integrity, configuring print options, and exporting database objects.

> To complete the practice tasks in this chapter, you need the practice files contained in the **MOSAccessExpert2019\Objective1** practice file folder. For more information, see "Download the practice files" in this book's Introduction.

Objective 1.1: Modify database structure

Import objects or data from other sources

Rather than you having to create tables, queries, forms, reports, macros, or modules from scratch, the object or data you need might already reside in another Access database. In that case, you can import one or more objects into your current Access database. If you import a table, you also have the option of linking to the data source, which means if the source changes, so does your version of the data.

See Also For more information on importing data into tables, see "Objective 2.1: Create tables." To learn more about linked tables, see "Create linked tables from external sources" in that same objective.

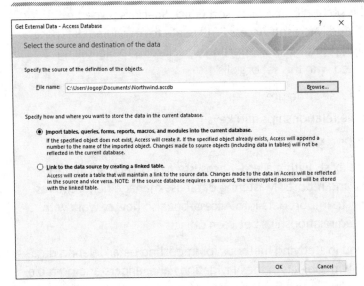

Importing objects from an Access database requires selecting the source data and how you want the objects imported.

You use the Import Objects dialog box to select what you want to import using the six tabs, one for each object type: Tables, Queries, Forms, Reports, Macros, and

Modules. On each tab, Access displays a list of the available objects of that type in the source data.

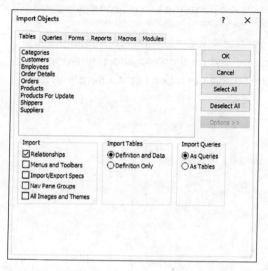

Options for importing database objects from an Access database.

Clicking the Options button displays the following importing options:

- **Import** The Relationships option determines whether table relationships are preserved in the import operation; selecting the Menus And Toolbars option imports any custom menus and toolbars from databases created in versions of Access prior to Access 2007; selecting Import/Export Specs includes any import or export specifications defined in the source database; selecting Nav Pane Groups imports any custom Navigation Pane groups set up in the source database; and selecting All Images And Themes includes these elements with the import.

- **Import Tables** Importing both the definition and data for a table means that you end up with the entire table object: its structure and all of its records. Importing just the definition means you end up with a table that has the same structure as the source table but does not contain any records.

- **Import Queries** Importing a query as a query imports just the query definition. The database must have a table of the same name as the one the query uses, with compatible fields. Importing a query as a table creates a new table with a datasheet that includes the query's results. Any records or fields the query definition excludes are excluded.

3

◇◇

Exam Strategy In the Access Expert exam, you need to know not only how to import data into Access, but also how to export data from Access to other formats. Therefore, be sure to also study the material in "Export objects to alternative formats" in "Objective 1.3: Print and export data."

◇◇

If you often perform a particular import operation, it can be time-consuming to repeat the import steps over and over. You can reduce time and effort by saving the steps. Doing so enables you to perform the import operation in the future with just a few mouse clicks.

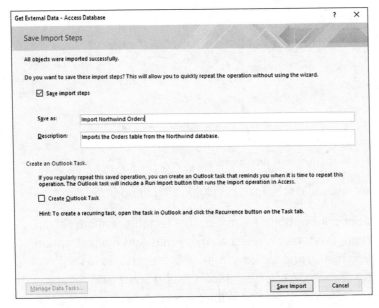

You can optionally save the steps for an import operation.

To import objects from an Access database

1. On the **External Data** tab, in the **Import & Link** group, click **New Data Source**.

2. Click **From Database**, then click **Access**. The **Get External Data – Access Database** dialog box opens.

3. In the **File name** text box, type the path and file name for the Access database file. Alternatively, click **Browse** to display the **File Open** dialog box, select the Access database file, and then click **Open**.

4. Select the **Import Tables, Queries, Forms, Reports, Macros, and Modules Into The Current Database** check box.

5. Click **OK**. The **Import Objects** dialog box opens.

6. Use the tabs to click each object you want to import. If you select an object by mistake, click it again to deselect it.

Tip Within each tab, you can quickly select every object in the tab by clicking Select All. To start over in a tab, click Deselect All.

---

7. Click **Options** to display the **Import** options at the bottom of the dialog box, then set the options for the import operation:

   - In the **Import** group, select the check box for each type of object you want to include in the import.

   - If you're importing one or more tables, in the **Import Tables** group, click **Definition And Data** or **Definition Only**.

   - If you're importing one or more queries, in the **Import Queries** area, click **As Queries** or **As Tables**.

8. Click **OK**. The **Save Import Steps** screen appears.

9. If you want to save the import steps, see the "To save import steps" procedure covered next. Otherwise, click **Close**. Access imports the objects into the database.

To save import steps

1. Perform an import, as shown in the "To import objects from an Access database" procedure, earlier in this task.

2. On the **Save Import Steps** screen of the operation, select **Save import steps**. Additional text boxes appear in the dialog box.

3. In the **Save As** text box, type a name for the saved import steps.

4. In the **Description** text box, type a description for the steps.

5. Select **Create Outlook Task** if you want Access to create an Outlook task that reminds you when it's time to run the import. The task includes a **Run Import** button that enables you to launch the import operation from Outlook.

Exam Strategy In the Access Expert exam, you might be asked to create a recurring Outlook task for running an import operation, so be sure you know how to modify the Outlook task so that it recurs on a regular schedule.

6. Click **Save Import**. Access saves the operation's steps. If you chose to create an Outlook task, the task opens in Outlook.

To run saved import steps

1. On the **External Data** tab, in the **Import & Link** group, click **Saved Imports**. The **Manage Data Tasks** dialog box opens with the **Saved Imports** tab displayed.

2. On the **Saved Imports** tab, click the import that you want to run.

    Tip If you didn't create an Outlook task for the import when you first ran the operation, you can do so from the Manage Data Tasks dialog box by clicking the import and then clicking Create Outlook Task.

3. Click **Run**. Access runs the import operation and then displays a message saying that the objects were imported successfully.

4. Click **OK** to return to the **Manage Data Tasks** dialog box.

5. Click **Close**.

Delete database objects

Database objects normally store important or useful information, so the person responsible for the database takes steps to keep that data safe. However, some objects become expendable over time because the data is now out of date, inaccurate, or redundant. In such cases, you can delete any object from your database—even tables that contain records.

IMPORTANT Be careful not to delete anything that you need to keep because it is not possible to undo an object deletion.

Access databases depend on the relationship between tables to preserve the integrity of data and to eliminate redundant data. You can delete most types of database objects, including queries, forms, and reports, without affecting underlying relationships. However, Access prevents you from deleting a table that is related to another table without first deleting the relationship. Access deletes the relationship for you if you agree.

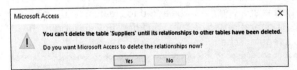

Access warns you that a table cannot be deleted until its relationships are removed.

See Also For more information about table relationships, see "Objective 1.2: Manage table relationships and keys."

To delete a database object

1. Close the object that you want to delete.

2. In the **Navigation Pane**, right-click the object, then click **Delete**.

3. In the **Microsoft Access** message box asking you to confirm that you want to delete the object and remove it from all groups, click **Yes**.

4. If you are deleting a table and Access prompts you to confirm that you want Access to delete the relationship, click **Yes** to remove the relationship and delete the table.

Hide and display objects in the Navigation Pane

This section focuses on the Access Navigation Pane and how you can modify and organize it to display different views of the objects in a database. The ability to modify the Navigation Pane means that it can serve the needs of a range of users—from a database's designer to its casual users.

For example, you can have multiple object types (tables, queries, forms, and so on) grouped under a heading such as Customers & Orders instead of headings such as Tables, Queries, and Forms. Headings such as Customers & Orders help clarify functional areas of the database and help users find forms and queries related to the area they are working with.

When you change how database objects are displayed in the Navigation Pane, you work with a menu that has several options. This menu arranges commands in two areas, marked by the shaded labels Navigate To Category and Filter By Group. The Navigate To Category area includes categories such as Object Type, Tables And Related Views, Created Date, and Modified Date. For each category, the Filter By Group area provides options that you can apply to display a subset of objects. For example, if you select Modified Date in the Navigate To Category area, you can then filter the list by selecting Today, Three Weeks Ago, Yesterday, Older, or All Dates. For the Object Type category, you can filter the Navigation Pane to view only objects of a specific type or view all objects.

The Tables And Related Views category displays each table in the database together with other database objects that depend on it. Using this view is helpful when you make changes to a table's design. For example, by choosing the Tables And Related Views category and then choosing a single table in the Filter By Group area, you can see which objects depend on the table, and you can review the design of those objects to be sure that the changes you want to make to the table won't affect the other objects in ways you don't intend.

You can also sort the list of objects in a category, showing them in ascending or descending order or by name, type, and date criteria. You can also change the level of detail that is shown for objects in the Navigation Pane. You can display a list of names with a small icon, show a larger icon next to the name of the object, or show details such as the created and modified date for the object.

You can set up Navigation Pane categories and groups of your own in the Navigation Options dialog box.

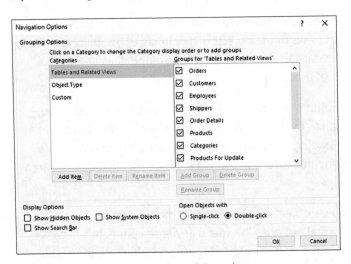

Organize the Navigation Pane into categories and groups.

The categories defined for the database appear in the list at the left, and each group defined for a category appears in the list at the right. You can hide a group from being displayed in the Navigation Pane, or select display options to show hidden and system objects in the Navigation Pane or to show or hide the search bar. By using the Open Objects With options, you can control whether an object opens when it is clicked (similar to a hyperlink) or double-clicked.

When you work with the default Custom category, the Groups For list includes a group named *Custom Group 1* and a group named *Unassigned Objects*, which is a built-in group that contains all the objects in a database.

Tip You can reposition a custom category or group by using the arrows that appear beside an item's name when you select it. You cannot place a custom category above the two built-in categories or place a custom group below the built-in group Unassigned Objects.

When you add a database object to a custom group, you add only a shortcut to that object, not the object itself. This means that you can delete a shortcut from a custom group without deleting the database object.

To create and modify Navigation Pane categories and groups

1. Right-click the **Navigation Pane** title bar, then click **Navigation Options**.

2. In the **Navigation Options** dialog box, do any of the following, then click **OK**:

   - To add a category, click **Add Item** and then enter a name for the category.

   - To rename the selected category, click **Rename Item**, edit the name, and then press **Enter**.

   - To delete the selected category, click **Delete Item**, and then in the message box asking you to confirm the deletion, click **OK**.

   - To add a group to the selected category, click **Add Group**, then enter a name for the group.

   - To rename the selected group, click **Rename Group**, edit the name, and then press **Enter**.

   - To delete the selected group, click **Delete Group**, and then in the message box asking you to confirm the deletion, click **OK**.

   Tip You can rename and delete only custom groups.

   - In the **Display Options** area, select or clear the check boxes for showing hidden objects, system objects, and the search bar.

   - In the **Open Objects With** area, click **Single-click** or **Double-click**.

To add objects to a group

1. In the **Navigation Pane**, display the category that contains the group.

2. In the **Unassigned Objects** group, right-click the object you want to add to the group, click **Add To Group**, and then select the group.

To hide an object in a group

→ In the **Navigation Pane**, right-click the object, then click **Hide In This Group**.

Objective 1.1 practice tasks

The practice file for these tasks is located in the **MOSAccessExpert2019\ Objective1** practice file folder. The folder also contains a result file that you can use to check your work. Save the results of the tasks in the same folder.

➤ From the Access Start screen or the New page of the Backstage view, do the following:

❑ Create a blank desktop database. (Depending on your installation of Access, the template might be named *Blank database* or *Blank desktop database*.) Name the database **MOSDatabase** and save it in the practice file folder.

❑ Import the Customers and Orders table definitions (not the data) from the **AccessExpert_1-1** database.

➤ Open the **AccessExpert_1-1** database and do the following:

❑ If the Info bar appears, click the *Enable Content* button.

❑ Delete the Table1 table.

❑ Create a Navigation Pane category named **Northwind**, and groups named **Customers**, **Products**, and **Employees**.

❑ Add the Customers, Order Details, Orders, and Shippers tables to the Customers group. Add the Categories, Products, and Suppliers tables to the Products group, and add the Employees table to the Employees group.

❑ Open the **AccessExpert_1-1_results** database. Compare the two databases to check your work. Then close the open databases.

Objective 1.2: Manage table relationships and keys

Most database applications (and *all* well-designed database applications) store their information in multiple tables. Although most of these tables have nothing to do with one another (for example, tables of customer information and employee payroll data), it's likely that at least some of the tables do contain related information (such as tables of customer information and customer orders).

Working with multiple, related tables presents you with two challenges: you need to design your database so that the related data is accessible, and you need to set up links between the tables so that the related information can be retrieved and worked with quickly and easily. This topic tackles both challenges and shows you how to exploit the full multiple-table powers of Access.

Set primary keys

It is advantageous to be able to uniquely identify each record. For example, if you have a Contacts table that has multiple entries for people named John Smith, how do you easily differentiate between them? In Access, you do this by designating a *primary key*, which is the field by which each record will be uniquely identified and by which relationships between tables can be created. You may use any field that you like for the primary key. You can use an AutoNumber field to allow Access to assign number-ing for you, or you can use a Number or Text field. The only limitations are that the field must contain a unique value for each record and it cannot be left blank. A table usually has only one primary key. When a unique combination of two or more fields' values forms the primary key, it is called a *composite key*.

You set the primary key for a table using Design view. Access designates the primary key by displaying a key icon to the left of the field name.

Access designates the primary key with a lock icon.

To open a table in Design view

➔ If the table is closed, right-click the table in the **Navigation Pane**, then click **Design View**.

➔ If the table is open in another view, on the **Design** tool tab, in the **Views** group, click **View**, then click **Design View**.

〰〰〰〰〰〰〰〰〰〰〰〰〰〰〰〰〰〰〰〰〰〰〰〰〰〰〰〰〰

Exam Strategy In the Access Expert exam, it is expected that you know how to switch between views for any database object, so be sure you are familiar with these methods, which can be generalized to any Access object.

〰〰〰〰〰〰〰〰〰〰〰〰〰〰〰〰〰〰〰〰〰〰〰〰〰〰〰〰〰

To set a primary key

1. Open the table in Design view.

2. Select the field or fields you want to designate as the table's primary key. To select multiple fields, press **Ctrl** and select the fields.

3. On the **Design** tool tab, in the **Tools** group, click **Primary Key**.

To remove the primary key designation from a field

1. Open the table in Design view.

2. Select the field or fields from which you want to remove the primary key designation.

3. On the **Design** tool tab, in the **Tools** group, click **Primary Key**.

Understand relationships

Why do you need to be concerned with multiple tables? Isn't it easier to work with one large table instead of two or three medium-sized ones? To answer these questions and demonstrate the problems that arise when you ignore relational database models, take a look at a simple example: a table of sales leads.

The following table outlines the structure of a simple table (named Leads) that stores data on sales leads.

Field	Description
LeadID	The primary key
FirstName	The contact's first name
LastName	The contact's last name

Field	Description
Company	The company that the contact works for
Address	The company's address
City	The company's city
State	The company's state
PostalCode	The company's postal or ZIP code
Phone	The contact's phone number
Fax	The contact's fax number
Source	Where the lead came from
Notes	Notes or comments related to the sales lead

This structure works fine until you need to add two or more leads from the same company (a not-uncommon occurrence). In this case, you end up with repeating information in the Company, Address, City, and State fields. (The PostalCode field also repeats, as do, in some cases, the Phone, Fax, and Source fields.)

All this repetition makes the table unnecessarily large, which is bad enough, but it also creates three major problems:

- During data entry, the repeated information must be entered for each lead from the same company.

- Entering the same data repeatedly increases the chances of entering that data either incorrectly (due to typos and other errors) or inconsistently (for example, entering **St.** in one field and **Street** in another).

- If any of the repeated information changes (such as the company's name or address), each corresponding record must be changed.

One way to eliminate the repetition and solve the data entry and maintenance ineffi-ciencies is to change the table's focus. As it stands, each record in the table identifies a specific contact in a company. But it's the company information that repeats, so it makes sense to allow only one record per company. You can then include separate fields for each sales lead within the company. The new structure might look something like the one shown in the following table.

Field	Description
LeadID	The primary key
Company	The company's name
Address	The company's address
City	The company's city
State	The company's state
PostalCode	The company's postal or ZIP code
Phone	The company's phone number
Fax	The company's fax number
First_1	The first name of contact #1
Last_1	The last name of contact #1
Source_1	Where the lead for contact #1 came from
Notes_1	Notes or comments related to contact #1
First_2	The first name of contact #2
Last_2	The last name of contact #2
Source_2	Where the lead for contact #2 came from
Notes_2	Notes or comments related to contact #2
First_3	The first name of contact #3
Last_3	The last name of contact #3
Source_3	Where the lead for contact #3 came from
Notes_3	Notes or comments related to contact #3

In this setup, the company information appears only once, and the contact-specific data (I'm assuming this involves only the first name, last name, source, and notes) appears in separate field groups (for example, First_1, Last_1, Source_1, and Notes_1). This setup solves the earlier problems, but at the cost of a new dilemma: the structure as it stands will hold only three sales leads per company. Of course, it's entirely conceivable that a large firm might have more than three contacts—perhaps even dozens. This raises two unpleasant difficulties:

- If you run out of repeating groups of contact fields, new ones must be added. Although this might not be a problem for the database designer, most data entry clerks generally don't have access to the table design (nor should they).

- Empty fields take up as much disk real estate as full ones, so making room for, say, a dozen contacts from one company means that all the records that have only one or two contacts have huge amounts of wasted space.

To solve the twin problems of repetition between records and repeated field groups within records, you need to turn to the relational database model. This model was developed by Dr. Edgar Codd of IBM in the early 1970s. It was based on a complex relational algebra theory, so the pure form of the rules and requirements for a true relational database setup is quite complicated and decidedly impractical for business applications. However, a simplified version of the model requires just three redesign steps:

1. Separate the data (discussed immediately following these steps).

2. Add foreign keys to the tables (see "Set foreign keys," later in this task).

3. Establish a link (that is, a relationship) between the related tables (see "Set relationships," later in this task).

After you know which fields you need to include in your database application, the first step in setting up a relational database is to divide these fields into separate tables where the "theme" of each table is unique. In technical terms, each table must be composed of only entities (that is, records) from a single *entity class*.

For example, the table of sales leads you saw earlier dealt with data that had two entity classes: the contacts and the companies for which they worked. Every one of the problems encountered with that table can be traced to the fact that we were trying to combine two entity classes into a single table. The first step toward a relational solution is to create separate tables for each class of data. To that end, the following shows the table structure of the contact data (the Contacts table):

Field	Description
ContactID	The primary key
FirstName	The contact's first name
LastName	The contact's last name

Field	Description
Phone	The contact's phone number
Fax	The contact's fax number
Source	Where the lead came from
Notes	Notes or comments related to the sales lead

And the following table shows the structure of the company information (the Companies table). Note, in particular, that both tables include a primary key field.

Field	Description
CompanyID	The primary key
CompanyName	The company's name
Address	The company's address
City	The company's city
State	The company's state
PostalCode	The company's postal or ZIP code
Phone	The company's phone number (main switchboard)

Set foreign keys

At first glance, separating the tables seems self-defeating because, if you've done the job properly, the two tables will have nothing in common. So, the second step in this relational redesign is to define the commonality between the tables.

In the sales leads example, what is the common ground between the Contacts and Companies tables? It's that every one of the leads in the Contacts table works for a specific firm in the Companies table. What's needed is some way of relating the appropriate information in Companies to each record in Contacts (without, of course, the inefficiency of simply cramming all the data into a single table, as we tried earlier).

The way you do this in relational database design is to establish a field that is common to both tables. You can then use this common field to set up a link between the two tables. The field you use must satisfy three conditions:

- It must not have the same name as an existing field in the other table.

- It must uniquely identify each record in the other table.

- To save space and reduce data entry errors, it must be the smallest field that satisfies the two preceding conditions.

In the sales leads example, you need to add a field to the Contacts table that establishes a link to the appropriate record in the Companies table. The CompanyName field uniquely identifies each firm, but it's too large to be of use. The Phone field is also a unique identifier and is smaller, but the Contacts table already has a Phone field. The best solution is to use CompanyID, the Companies table's primary key field. The following table shows the revised structure of the Contacts table that includes the CompanyID field.

Field	Description
ContactID	The primary key
CompanyID	The Companies table foreign key
FirstName	The contact's first name
LastName	The contact's last name
Phone	The contact's phone number
Fax	The contact's fax number
Source	Where the lead came from
Notes	Notes or comments related to the sales lead

When a table includes a primary key field from a related database, the field is called a *foreign key*. Foreign keys are the secret to successful relational database design.

To set a foreign key in a table

1. Open the table in Design view.

2. In the **Field Name** column, enter the name of the foreign key field.

3. In the **Data Type** column, select the data type that matches the data type of the field in the other table (usually **Number**).

4. Save the changes to the table.

Understand relational database models

Depending on the data you're working with, you can set up one of several relational database models. In each of these models, however, you must differentiate between a *child* table (also called a *dependent* table or a *controlled* table) and a *parent* table (also called a *primary* table or a *controlling* table). The child table is the one that is dependent on the parent table to fill in the definition of its records. The Contacts table, for example, is a child table because it is dependent on the Companies table for the company information associated with each person.

You should consider three main relational database models:

- **One-to-many** The most common relational model is one where a single record in the parent table relates to multiple records in the child table. This is called a *one-to-many* relationship. The sales leads example is a one-to-many relationship because one record in the Companies table can relate to many records in the Contacts table (in other words, you can have multiple sales contacts from the same firm). In these models, the "many" table is the one where you add the foreign key. Another example of a one-to-many relationship is an application that tracks accounts receivable invoices. You need one table for the invoice data (Invoices) and another for the customer data (Customers). In this case, one customer can place many orders, so Customers is the parent table, Invoices is the child table, and the common field is the Customer table's primary key.

- **One-to-one** If your data requires that one record in the parent table be related to only one record in the child table, you have a *one-to-one* model. The most common use of one-to-one relationships is to create separate entity classes to enhance security. In a hospital, for example, each patient's data is a single entity class, but it makes sense to create separate tables for the patient's basic information (such as the name and address) and medical history. This setup enables you to add extra levels of security to the confidential medical data (such as a password). The two tables then become related based on a common PatientID key field. Another example of a one-to-one model is employee data. You separate the less sensitive information such as job title and startup date into one table and restricted information such as salary and commissions into a second table. If each employee has a unique identification number, you use that number to set up a relationship between the two tables. Note that in a one-to-one model, the concepts of *child* and *parent* tables are interchangeable. Each table relies on the other to form the complete picture of each patient or employee.

- **Many-to-many** In some cases, you might have data in which many records in one table can relate to many records in another table. This is called a *many-to-many* relationship. In this case, there is no direct way to establish a common field between the two tables. To see why, consider an accounts receivable application, which might include a table of invoice data and a table of product information. The idea here is that a given product can appear in many invoices and any given invoice can contain many products. This is a many-to-many relationship, and it implies that *both* tables are parents (or, to put it another way, neither table is directly dependent on the other). But relational theory says that a child table is needed to establish a common field. In this case, the solution is to set up a third table—called a *linking table* (or sometimes a *junction table* or *relation table*—that is the child of both the original tables. In the example, the relation table contains the detail data for each invoice, as well as foreign keys from both Invoices (InvoiceID) and Products (ProductID). The following shows a simplified example of a linking table:

Field	Description
DetailID	The primary key
InvoiceID	The foreign key from the Invoices table
ProductID	The foreign key from the Products table
Quantity	The quantity ordered

After you have your foreign keys inserted into your tables, the final step in designing your relational model is to establish a link between the two tables. This step is covered in the next section.

Set relationships

Now that you know the theory behind the relational model, you can turn your attention to creating and working with relationships between tables, which is what this section is all about. In Access, you use the Relationships window to create and manage relationships between tables.

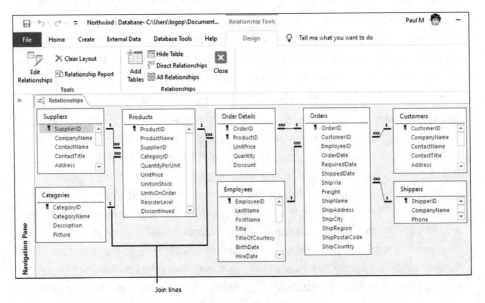

You use the Relationships window to establish relations between tables.

Observe the lines that connect each table in the Relationships window. These lines are called *join lines* and each join line connects the two fields that contain the related information. For example, the Suppliers and Products tables are joined on the common SupplierID field. In this case, SupplierID is the primary key field for the Suppliers table, and it appears as a foreign key in the Products table. This connection lets you relate any product to its corresponding supplier data.

The symbols attached to the join lines tell you the type of relation. In the join between the Suppliers and Products tables, for example, the Suppliers side of the join line has a 1, and the Products side of the line has an infinity symbol (∞). This stands for "many," so you interpret this join as a one-to-many relation.

Access lets you set up two main types of joins:

- **Inner join** An *inner join* includes only those records in which the related fields in the two tables match each other exactly (which is why this type of join is often called an *equijoin*). This is the most common type of join.

- **Outer join** An *outer join* includes every record from one of the tables and only those records from the other table in which the related fields match each other exactly. In the sales leads example, it's possible that there might be companies for which no contacts have yet been established. Creating an inner join between the Company and Contacts tables shows you only those firms that have existing contacts. However, setting up an outer join shows *all* the records in the Companies table, including those in which there is no corresponding record in the Contacts table.

An outer join is also called a *left-outer join*. To see why, consider a one-to-many relation. Here, the "left" side is the "one" table, and the "right" side is the "many" table. So, this type of join includes every record from the one (left) side and only those matching records from the many (right) side. You use the term *left-outer join* when you need to differentiate it from a *right-outer join*. In a one-to-many relationship, this type of join includes every record from the many (right) side and only those matching records from the one (left) side.

If you need to establish a new relationship between two tables, you open the Relationships window, add the tables, create the relationship, and then specify the details using the Edit Relationships dialog box.

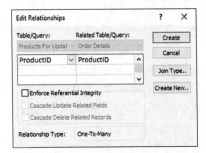

You use the Edit Relationships dialog box to configure a relationship between two tables.

In Access, a table's *dependencies* are those database objects that rely on data from the table. For example, an Orders table might depend on data from a Customers table because you have set up a relationship between them. Similarly, queries or forms may depend on the table.

You can view an object's dependencies from the Object Dependencies task pane. This is easier than trying to decipher the relationships in the Relationships window, particularly in a complex database. The Relationships window does not need to be open for you to view object dependencies.

Tip Viewing an object's dependencies in Access requires that you enable the Name AutoCorrect feature, which tracks object name changes. On the File tab, click Options, click the Current Database tab, select the Track Name AutoCorrect Info check box, and then click OK when Access asks you to confirm. Click OK to close the Access Options dialog box, then close and reopen the database when Access prompts you.

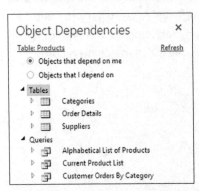

You use the Object Dependencies pane to see which objects have a relationship with the selected object.

To open the Relationships window

→ On the **Database Tools** tab, in the **Relationships** group, click **Relationships**.

To display tables in the Relationships window

1. On the **Design** tool tab, in the **Relationships** group, click **Add Tables**.

2. In the **Show Table** dialog box, select the tables, then click **Add**.

Tip Hold down the Ctrl key to select multiple tables.

To remove tables from the Relationships window

→ In the **Relationships** window, do either of the following:

- To remove one table, click the table to select it. Then on the **Design** tool tab, in the **Relationships** group, click **Hide Table**.

- To remove all tables, on the **Design** tool tab, in the **Tools** group, click **Clear Layout**.

To display relationships in the Relationships window

→ In the **Relationships** window, do either of the following:

- To display all direct relationships of a specific table, click the table to select it. Then on the **Design** tool tab, in the **Relationships** group, click **Direct Relationships**.

- To display all relationships in the database, on the **Design** tool tab, in the **Relationships** group, click **All Relationships**.

To create a table relationship

1. Open the **Relationships** window. If the tables you want to create relationships between aren't displayed in the **Relationships** window, add them.

2. Arrange the table boxes so that in each box you can see the fields you want to use for the join.

3. Drag the related field from one table and drop it on the related field in the other table. Access displays the **Edit Relationships** dialog box.

4. The grid should show the names of the fields in each table that you want to relate. If not, click the arrow to use the list in one or both cells to click the correct field or fields.

5. To set the type of join, click **Join Type** to display the **Join Properties** dialog box. Here, option 1 corresponds to an inner join, option 2 corresponds to a left-outer join, and option 3 corresponds to a right-outer join. After you've clicked the option you want, click **OK** to return to the **Edit Relationships** dialog box.

You use the Join Properties dialog box to specify the join type for the relationship.

See Also For information on enforcing referential integrity, see "Enforce referential integrity," later in this task.

6. Click **Create**. Access establishes the relationship and displays a join line between the two fields.

To modify a relationship

1. Open the **Relationships** window and do either of the following:

   - Click the relationship line between two tables. Then on the **Design** tool tab, in the **Tools** group, click **Edit Relationship**.

   - Right-click the relationship line between two tables, then click **Edit Relationship**.

2. In the **Edit Relationships** dialog box, modify the table or query selections, the join type, or the options, and then click **OK**.

To remove a relationship

→ If you no longer need a join, you can remove it by clicking the join line and pressing **Delete**, or by right-clicking the join line and then clicking **Delete**. When Access asks you to confirm the deletion, click **Yes**.

To view an object's dependencies

1. If the **Relationships** window is open, on the **Design** tab, in the **Relationships** group, click **Close**, then click **Yes** if Access prompts you to save the layout.

2. In the **Navigation** Pane, click the object that you want to examine.

3. On the **Database Tools** tab, in the **Relationships** group, click **Object Dependencies**. Access displays the **Object Dependencies** task pane.

4. Select the type of dependency you want to view:

   - **Objects that depend on me** Select this option to see objects that get data from the object you chose in step 2.

   - **Objects that I depend on** Select this option to see objects from which the object you chose in step 2 gets data.

Enforce referential integrity

Database applications that work with multiple, related tables need to enforce *referential integrity rules*. These rules ensure that related tables remain in a consistent state relative to one another.

One cause of integrity loss in a database is when you make changes to a primary key value in the parent table. If that new key value isn't also applied to each child table, then the relationship between the parent table and its child tables is broken. For example, if you change a CompanyID value in the Companies table, all related records in the Contacts table should have their CompanyID fields updated.

Another cause of integrity loss is when you delete a record in a parent table but you don't also delete the related records on all child tables. In the sales leads application, for example, suppose the Companies table includes an entry for "ACME Coyote Supplies" and that the Contacts table contains three leads who work for ACME. What would happen if you deleted the ACME Coyote Supplies record from the Companies table? The three records in the Contacts table would no longer be related to any record in the Companies table. Child records without corresponding records in the parent table are called, appropriately enough, *orphans*. This situation leaves your tables in an inconsistent state, which can have unpredictable consequences. For example, certain types of queries may fail because Access can't properly relate the underlying tables.

Applying primary key parent table changes to child tables and preventing orphaned records is what is meant by enforcing referential integrity.

To enforce referential integrity

1. Either create, but don't complete, a relationship between two tables, or edit an existing relationship.

2. In the **Edit Relationships** dialog box, select the **Enforce Referential Integrity** check box.

3. Select the **Cascade Update Related Fields** check box if, when you make changes to a primary key value in the parent table, you want Access to update the new key value for all related records in all child tables.

4. Select the **Cascade Delete Related Fields** check box if, when you delete a record from the parent table, you want Access to delete all related records in all child tables.

5. Click **Create** (for a new relationship) or **OK** (for an edited relationship).

Objective 1.2 practice tasks

The practice file for these tasks is located in the **MOSAccess2016\Objective1** practice file folder. The folder also contains a result file that you can use to check your work.

➤ Open the **AccessExpert_1-2** database from the practice file folder, then do the following:

❑ If the Info bar appears, click the Enable Content button.

❑ Open the Categories table in Design view.

❑ Set the CategoryID field as the table's primary key.

❑ Save your changes and then close the table.

❑ Open the Suppliers table in Design view.

❑ Set the SupplierID field as the table's primary key.

❑ Save your changes, then close the table.

❑ Open the Products table in Design view.

❑ Set the ProductsID field as the table's primary key.

❑ Add two foreign keys to the Products table: CategoryID and SupplierID (use the Number data type for both).

❑ Save your changes, then close the table.

➤ Open the Relationships window and do the following:

❑ Add the Categories and Products tables in the window.

❑ Create a relationship between the Category table (CategoryID field) and the Products table (CategoryID field).

❑ Edit the relationship between the Category table and the Products table to enforce referential integrity.

❏ Use the Add Tables command to add the Suppliers table to the Relationships window.

❏ Create a relationship between the Suppliers table (SupplierID field) and the Products table (SupplierID field).

❏ Edit the relationship between the Suppliers table and the Products table to enforce referential integrity.

➤ Open the **Access_1-2_results** database. Compare the two databases to check your work, then close the open databases.

Objective 1.3: Print and export data

You can use the data you store in Access in several ways. Within Access, you can create reports, for example, and distribute the reports in printed or electronic format. You can also export data to formats that are compatible with earlier versions of Access and with other programs, including Microsoft Excel and Word.

This topic first focuses on how to print reports and specific database records. It then describes how to export data from Access.

Configure print options for records, forms, and reports

When you print a table, query, form, or report, you can send the data directly to the default printer (without setting any printing options), use the Print dialog box to select a printer and set printing options, or work in print preview, a view that enables you to refine the layout, view the data in different ways, and export the data.

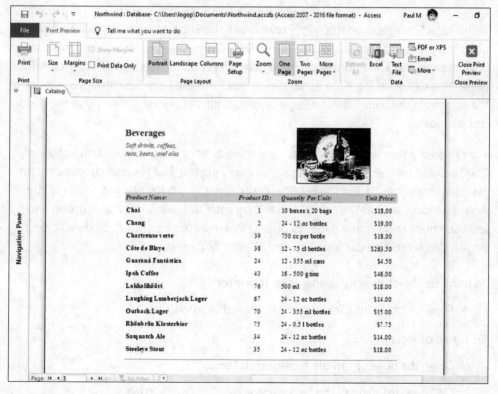

A report open in print preview.

The Print dialog box provides standard options with which you can specify a page range, set the number of copies, and adjust the page setup. It also provides an option for printing selected records. You must select the records you want to print before opening the Print dialog box. In general, you will print records that you select in a table or query that is open in Datasheet view.

In print preview, Access provides commands to adjust page size and margins, change the page layout and page orientation (switching from portrait to landscape, for example), set up the printout in columns, and view the printout by zooming in and out or by displaying one or more pages. With these views, you can assess whether the printout's formatting is consistent, for example, or whether any important data might be missing. Many of the commands on the Print Preview tab are also available when you design and format a report in Design view or Layout view.

Tip The Print Preview tab also provides a set of options (in the Data group) for exporting data to other programs or in various formats. These options are described in "Export objects to alternative formats" later in this topic.

In the Page Size group on the Print Preview tab, the Show Margins option displays or hides the printout's margins, and the Print Data Only option removes elements such as column headings and information in page headers and footers that Access normally prints. You can open the Page Setup dialog box from the Page Size group, but many of the options in the Page Size and Page Layout groups duplicate options that the dialog box provides.

The range of zoom levels in print preview extends from 10 percent to a maximum of 1,000 percent (not all zoom levels apply to every object), but you can choose only pre-set options (such as 75% or 200%). The Zoom slider, in the lower-right corner of the Access window, adjusts the zoom level with greater flexibility. The Zoom group also lets you choose how many pages to display in a multipage printout. By default, one page is displayed. You can also display 2, 4, 8, or 12 pages.

To print an object directly to the default printer

→ For a report, right-click the report, then click **Print**.

Or, for all objects

1. Open the object from the **Navigation Pane**.

2. On the **Print** page of the Backstage view, click **Quick Print**.

To set printing options and print an object

1. Open the report from the **Navigation Pane**.

2. On the **Print** page of the Backstage view, click **Print**.

3. In the **Print** dialog box, set options for the print range, number of copies, and other printer properties. Then click **OK**.

To print selected records from a table or a query

1. Open the table or query in Datasheet view.

2. Select the records you want to print.

3. On the **Print** page of the Backstage view, click **Print** to open the **Print** dialog box.

4. In the **Print range** area, click **Selected Records**. (If you don't click **Selected Records**, Access prints all the records in the datasheet.)

5. Click **OK**.

To manage print and page setup options for a database object in print preview

1. Open the database object you want to print if it is not already open.

2. On the **Print** page of the Backstage view, click **Print Preview**.

3. In the **Page Size** group, adjust paper size and margins and specify whether only data should be printed.

4. In the **Page Layout** group, set the page orientation, columns, and other page setup options.

5. In the **Print** group, click **Print**.

6. In the **Print** dialog box, set options for the number of copies and other printing options, and then click **OK**.

Export objects to alternative formats

One of the advantages of entering and maintaining data in a database is the capability to make the data available in other formats. For example, you can export data to use it in other programs and in other contexts. Data related to sales, budgets, orders, and other financial records can be exported to Excel for analysis. A list of contacts can be exported to a list in a SharePoint site or used in a mail merge in Word. Exporting data to a text file or to an XML file puts the data in a format that is compatible with other database and spreadsheet programs, and creating a PDF or an XPS file by using an export operation lets you distribute data in formats designed for review instead of analysis and editing.

The Export dialog box provides options to maintain an object's formatting and layout when you export it, view the exported file when the operation is complete, and export only selected records (in lieu of the complete record set that is contained in a specific table or query, for example). Specific operations, such as exporting to a text file, require you to set additional options that control where and how data is exported. You can also save export settings and then repeat an export operation in a single step.

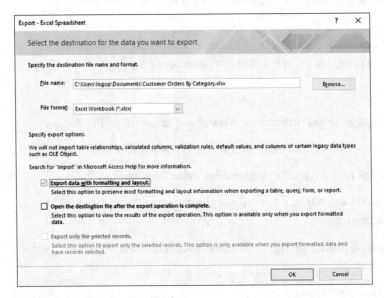

Exporting data to an Excel workbook.

The default setting for exporting data to Excel is the Excel Workbook file format (.xlsx). The options you can choose for a file format depend on the type of object you export. When you export records from a query, for example, you can keep Excel Workbook (.xlsx) or choose Excel Binary Workbook, Microsoft Excel 5.0/95 Workbook, or Excel 97–Excel 2003 Workbook. If you export a report, the file formats are limited to Microsoft Excel 5.0/95 Workbook and Excel 97–Excel 2003 Workbook.

The availability of export options also depends on the type of object. If you export a report, the Export Data With Formatting And Layout check box is selected by

1

default and cannot be cleared. If you export a query or a table, you can select or clear the formatting and layout check box. By selecting that check box, you can open the destination file, and if you selected a subset of the records, you can then select the option to export only those records.

If you export an object's complete record set, Access displays another dialog box, which has an option for saving the export steps. Saving the export steps saves time if you expect to run this export operation again using the same object and the same export settings.

When you export data to a text file, the steps you follow depend on whether you select the Export Data With Formatting And Layout option. When you select this option, Access displays the Encode As dialog box, which provides a choice of encoding schemes: Windows (Default), MS-DOS, Unicode, or Unicode (UTF-8). The Windows (Default) and MS-DOS options apply to text files that will be used only in programs that support these formats. Most programs consuming text files can use files encoded with the Unicode option. Unicode (UTF-8) is a format used widely on the web.

If you don't select the Export Data With Formatting And Layout option, Access displays the Export Text Wizard. In export operations that rely on the Export Text Wizard, you specify whether to export the data as a delimited text file or as a fixed-width text file.

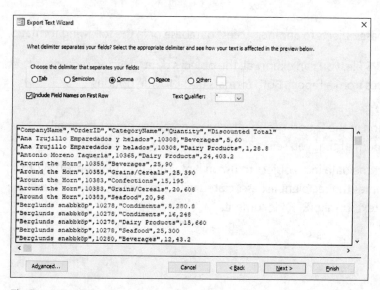

The Export Text Wizard.

From this point, the Export Text Wizard displays screens that refine your initial choice. For example, for delimited text files, you specify the character that separates fields in each record (often a comma), whether to include field names in the first row of the exported file, and the text qualifier character (which is used to handle instances of the delimiting character that appear in actual values). For fixed-width exports, you use the wizard to indicate where field breaks occur by dragging lines to create columns.

When you export data to an XML file, you have the option to also export the schema for the data (an XSD file) and the presentation of the data (which is defined in an XSL file). For the data, you can export records in related tables in addition to the data in the object you selected. You can also specify an encoding scheme (UTF-8 or UTF-16). Among the options related to exporting the schema are whether to include table and field properties and whether to embed the schema in the XML file or create a separate schema document. Presentation options include the location where the XLS file is stored, where related images are stored, and whether the XSL transformation is run from a client or a server computer. In the Run From area, the Client option creates an HTML file on the local computer that programmatically merges the XSL file and the data (XML) file. This option does not embed the presentation information in the data, which lets you update either the XSL file or the XML file without having to run the export operation again. The Server (ASP) option creates an Active Server Pages (ASP) file that merges the presentation with the data and sends the HTML file that is created to the local computer.

You can export database objects to another Access database or in the following formats:

- For a PDF or XPS file, you can export all the object's data, selected records, or specific pages from a report. Both formats also provide options for accessibility.
- The Email option in the Export group attaches a database object to email messages in a format that you select.
- You can export the data in an object to use in a mail-merge operation in Word (the data becomes the recipient list associated with the mail merge) or save the data as a rich-text format (RTF) document.

If you expect to use an export operation regularly, you can save the export steps you defined. By saving the export steps, you can run the operation in a single step.

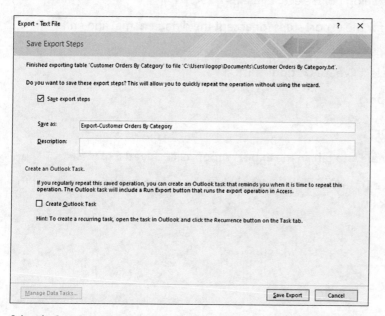

Select the Save Export Steps check box to later perform the export in a single step.

When you want to run a saved export in Access, on the External Data tab, in the Export group, click Saved Exports. Access opens the Manage Data Tasks dialog box. This dialog box provides options to run the export, create an Outlook task, modify the name or description provided earlier, and delete any saved exports (or saved imports) that you no longer need.

To export data from Access

1. In the **Navigation Pane**, select the object that contains the data you want to export.

2. On the **External Data** tab, in the **Export** group, click the format or program you want to export to.

3. In the **Export** dialog box, specify the file name and location, and select the export options you want to use: to include formatting and layout, to view the exported file, and to export only selected records.

4. Depending on the export option you select in step 2, use the options in the dialog boxes and the wizards Access provides to specify file format and related export options.

To save export steps

1. In the **Export** dialog box, select **Save export steps**.

2. Enter a name for the export steps (or accept the default name) and enter a description.

3. If you want, select **Create Outlook Task**.

4. Click **Save Export**.

To run a saved export

1. On the **External Data** tab, in the **Export** group, click **Saved Exports**.

2. In the **Manage Data Tasks** dialog box, select the export operation you want to run, then click **Run**.

Objective 1.3 practice tasks

The practice file for these tasks is located in the **MOSAccessExpert2019\ Objective1** practice file folder. The folder also contains a result file that you can use to check your work.

➤ Open the **AccessExpert_1-3** database from the practice file folder and do the following:

❏ If the Info bar appears, click the *Enable Content* button.

❏ Open the Customers report from the Navigation Pane, and then display the report in print preview. Change the margins to Wide.

❏ Export the Customers report to Word (use the Rich Text format option).

❏ Export the Customers table to Excel.

➤ Open the **AccessExpert_1-3_results** database. Compare the two databases to check your work, then close the open databases.

Objective group 2

Create and modify tables

The skills tested in this section of the Microsoft Office Specialist Expert exam for Microsoft Access 365 and Microsoft Access 2019 relate to creating and managing tables. Specifically, the following objectives are associated with this set of skills:

2.1 Create tables

2.2 Manage tables

2.3 Manage table records

2.4 Create and modify fields

When you create a database, Access automatically creates a new table that you can use to enter data by hand. You can also create your own tables as needed. However, for many database applications the data already resides in some other format, such as an Excel spreadsheet, an HTML document, a text or XML file, or another database. In that case, it's easier and faster to import the data from its current format to an Access table. You can either create a copy of the external data or you can set up a link between the original data and your Access table, which means that changes made to the external data are also propagated to the Access version of the data.

This chapter guides you in studying methods for importing data into tables, managing tables and records in tables, and creating and modifying fields.

> To complete the practice tasks in this chapter, you need the practice files contained in the **MOSAccessExpert2019\Objective2** practice file folder. For more information, see "Download the practice files" in this book's Introduction.

Objective 2.1: Create tables

If the data you want to work with resides in an external data source—usually a local file, a remote file (on a network or on the Internet), or data on a server—you need to import it into Access. Depending on the type of data source you are using, Access gives you one or more of the following choices for importing the data:

- **Import the source data into a new table in the current database.** Access either creates a new table to hold the data or replaces any data in an existing table. No link is maintained with the original data.

- **Append a copy of the records to an existing table.** Access adds the source data to the existing table. If the table does not exist, Access creates it. No link is maintained with the original data.

- **Link to the data source by creating a linked table.** Access adds the source data to the new table. A link is maintained with the original data, so if that data changes, the changes are reflected in the Access version of the data.

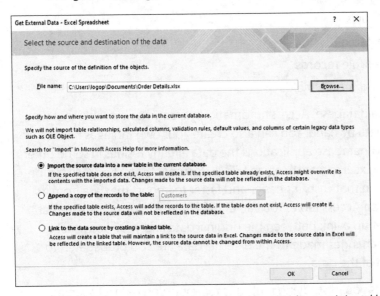

With most external data, you can import into a new table, append to an existing table, or link to the data source.

Access 365 and Access 2019 support a number of external data sources, including the following: Excel workbooks, HTML documents, XML files, text files, Access databases, and Outlook folders.

See Also For information about appending data to a table, see "Append records from external data," later in this task. For information about creating linked tables, see "Create linked tables from external sources," later in this task.

Import data into a new table

When you import data from Excel into a new table, the Import Spreadsheet Wizard prompts you for information to complete the operation. The wizard first prompts you for the worksheet or the named range you want to import. You can view the sample data that the wizard displays from the worksheet, but you cannot modify it. Access can use the column headings in the worksheet as field names in the database. You can also specify each field's data type and whether Access should index the field. The wizard's fourth page provides options for setting the table's primary key. Access can create an ID field in the table to use as the primary key, or you can select a primary key field or use no primary key in the new table.

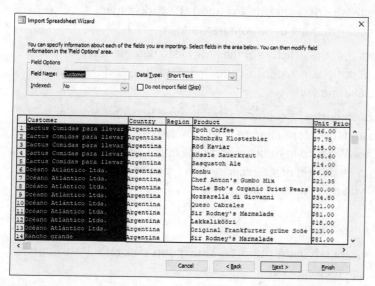

Define field names and data types when you import data from a spreadsheet.

See Also For information about running saved import and export operations, see "Objective 1.3: Print and export data."

You can import data from a text file that uses the .txt, .csv, .tab, or .asc file name extension. When you import data from a text file, you work with the Import Text Wizard. In the wizard, you first need to specify whether a character separates the fields of data in the text file (a delimited text file) or whether the data is arranged in fixed-width columns. For delimited text files, you must specify which character is used as the delimiter; for fixed-width files, you indicate where column breaks should occur.

The later pages of the Import Text Wizard are similar to those you work with in the Import Spreadsheet Wizard. You can name fields, specify a data type, indicate whether the field should be indexed, and skip a specific field. The wizard also prompts you to set up a primary key for the table.

Three of the other formats you can import are as follows:

- **HTML documents** Data is often available in documents created using HTML (Hypertext Markup Language), which is the language used to build web pages. Although this data is usually text, some HTML data comes either as a table (a rectangular array of rows and columns) or as preformatted text (text that has been structured with a predefined spacing used to organize data into columns with fixed widths). Both types are suitable for import into Access so that you can perform more extensive data analysis. To import HTML document data, the file must reside on your computer or on your network.

- **XML files** Access uses the structure of the XML file to determine table names and fields. Import options include Structure Only, Structure And Data, and Append Data To Existing Table(s).

- **Outlook folders** Importing a contacts or tasks folder from Outlook is an effective way to add this information to a database. Access runs the Import Exchange/Outlook Wizard when you import data from Outlook. The wizard prompts you to provide field names, specify data types, and set up indexes. You can skip fields if you don't want to import them.

To import Excel data into a table

1. On the **External Data** tab, in the **Import & Link** group, click **New Data Source**, click **From File**, and then click **Excel**.

2. In the **Get External Data – Excel Spreadsheet** dialog box, click **Import The Source Data Into A New Table In The Current Database**, click **Browse** to locate the source file, and then click **OK**.

3. In the **Import Spreadsheet Wizard**, select the data you want to import, then click **Next**:

   - To import the data from a worksheet, select **Show Worksheets**, then click the worksheet name.

   - To import the data from a named range, select **Show Named Ranges**, then click the range name.

4. If the first row of the Excel data contains headings and you want Access to use those headings as the field names for the new table, select the **First Row Contains Column Headings** check box, then click **Next**.

   IMPORTANT Your Excel headings might contain one or more characters that are illegal to use for Access field names, including the period (.), exclamation mark (!), and brackets ([and]). That's not a problem because Access will delete any illegal characters (and display a message to that effect) when it creates the field names.

   ---

5. On the next **Import Spreadsheet Wizard** page, click the field you want to work with, then edit the field name, select the data type, and specify whether you want the field indexed. Alternatively, you can select the **Do Not Import (Skip)** check box to tell Access to skip the field when importing the data.

6. Repeat step 5 for each field, then click **Next**.

7. On the next **Import Spreadsheet Wizard** page, select a primary key option, then click **Next**:

   - **Let Access Add Primary Key** Select this option to have Access create a new field named ID that acts as the primary key by using the AutoNumber data type.

   - **Choose My Own Primary Key** Select this option, then use the associated list to select the field you want to use as the primary key. Note that the field you choose must contain unique entries.

   - **No Primary Key** Select this option to skip adding a primary key to the new table.

8. On the final **Import Spreadsheet Wizard** page, type a name for your new table, then click **Finish** to return to the **Get External Data – Excel Spreadsheet** dialog box.

9. If you want to save the steps in this operation, select **Save Import Steps**, then click **Save Import**; otherwise, click **Close**.

To import HTML document data into a table

1. On the **External Data** tab, in the **Import & Link** group, click **New Data Source**, click **From File**, and then click **HTML Document**.

2. In the **Get External Data – HTML Document** dialog box, click **Import The Source Data Into A New Table In The Current Database**, click **Browse** to locate the source file, and then click **OK**.

3. In the **Import HTML Wizard**, if the first row of the HTML data contains headings and you want Access to use those headings as the field names for the new table, select the **First Row Contains Column Headings** check box, then click **Next**.

4. On the next **Import HTML Wizard** page, click the field you want to work with, then edit the field name, select the data type, and specify whether you want the field indexed. Alternatively, you can select the **Do Not Import (Skip)** check box to tell Access to skip the field when importing the data.

5. Repeat step 4 for each field, then click **Next**.

6. On the next **Import HTML Wizard** page, select a primary key option, then click **Next**:

   - **Let Access Add Primary Key** Select this option to have Access create a new field named ID that acts as the primary key by using the AutoNumber data type.

   - **Choose My Own Primary Key** Select this option and then use the associated list to select the field you want to use as the primary key. Note that the field you choose must contain unique entries.

   - **No Primary Key** Select this option to skip adding a primary key to the new table.

7. On the final **Import HTML Wizard** page, type a name for your new table, then click **Finish** to return to the **Get External Data – HTML Document** dialog box.

8. If you want to save the steps in this operation, select **Save Import Steps**, then click **Save Import**; otherwise, click **Close**.

To import XML data into a table

1. On the **External Data** tab, in the **Import & Link** group, click **New Data Source**, click **From File**, and then click **XML File**.

2. In the **Get External Data – XML File** dialog box, click **Browse** to locate the source file, then click **OK**.

3. In the **Import XML** dialog box, in the **Import Options** group, select how you want the XML data imported, then click **OK**:

   - **Structure Only** Select this option to import just the field names.

   - **Structure and Data** Select this option to import both the field name and the data.

   - **Append Data to Existing Table(s)** Select this option to add the data to an existing table (or tables, if the XML file contains multiple tables).

4. If you want to save the steps in this operation, select **Save Import Steps**, then click **Save Import**; otherwise, click **Close**.

To import text data into a table

1. On the **External Data** tab, in the **Import & Link** group, click **New Data Source**, click **From File**, and then click **Text File**.

2. In the **Get External Data – Text File** dialog box, click **Import The Source Data Into A New Table In The Current Database**, click **Browse** to locate the source file, and then click **OK**. The **Import Text Wizard** appears.

3. Select the type of text file you're importing:

   - **Delimited** Select this option if your text file uses a character (such as a comma) to separate each field, then click **Next**. Select the option that represents the character used in the source data to separate the fields (or select **Other** and then type the character in the text box). If the first row of the text data contains headings and you want Access to use those headings as the field names for the new table, select the **First Row Contains Column Headings** check box. Click **Next**.

   - **Fixed Width** Select this option if your text file uses a set width for each column of data, then click **Next**. Use the next **Import Text Wizard** page to adjust the column breaks as needed, then click **Next**.

4. On the next **Import Text Wizard** page, click the field you want to work with, then edit the field name, select the data type, and specify whether you want the field indexed. Alternatively, you can select the **Do Not Import (Skip)** check box to tell Access to skip the field when importing the data.

5. Repeat step 4 for each field, then click **Next**.

2

6. On the next **Import Text Wizard** page, select a primary key option, then click **Next**:

- **Let Access Add Primary Key** Select this option to have Access create a new field named ID that acts as the primary key by using the AutoNumber data type.

- **Choose My Own Primary Key** Select this option and then use the associated list to select the field you want to use as the primary key. Note that the field you choose must contain unique entries.

- **No Primary Key** Select this option to skip adding a primary key to the new table.

7. On the final **Import Text Wizard** page, type a name for your new table, then click **Finish** to return to the **Get External Data – Text File** dialog box.

8. If you want to save the steps in this operation, select **Save Import Steps**, then click **Save Import**; otherwise, click **Close**.

To import Outlook folder data into a table

1. On the **External Data** tab, in the **Import & Link** group, click **New Data Source**, click **From Other Sources**, and then click **Outlook Folder**.

2. In the **Get External Data – Outlook Folder** dialog box, click **Import The Source Data Into A New Table In The Current Database**, then click **OK**.

3. In the **Import Exchange/Outlook Wizard**, select the data you want to import, then click **Next**.

4. On the next **Import Exchange/Outlook Wizard** page, click the field you want to work with, then edit the field name, select the data type, and specify whether you want the field indexed. Alternatively, you can select the **Do Not Import (Skip)** check box to tell Access to skip the field when importing the data.

5. Repeat step 4 for each field, then click **Next**.

6. On the next **Import Exchange/Outlook Wizard** page, select a primary key option, then click **Next**:

- **Let Access Add Primary Key** Select this option to have Access create a new field named ID that acts as the primary key by using the AutoNumber data type.

- **Choose My Own Primary Key** Select this option and then use the associated list to select the field you want to use as the primary key. Note that the field you choose must contain unique entries.

- **No Primary Key** Select this option to skip adding a primary key to the new table.

7. On the final **Import Exchange/Outlook Wizard** page, type a name for your new table, then click **Finish** to return to the **Get External Data – Outlook Folder** dialog box.

8. If you want to save the steps in this operation, select **Save Import Steps**, then click **Save Import**; otherwise, click **Close**.

Append records from external data

When you import data from an Excel spreadsheet, an HTML document, a text file, or an Outlook folder, you can choose an option to append records to an existing table. Access adds the records in the source data to the table you specify. The steps for importing the data are then essentially the same as when you import data into a new table.

See Also For more information about importing data, see "Import data into a new table," earlier in this task.

To avoid errors when you append data, make sure that the external data source organization matches the structure of the table you are appending records to. For example, in an Excel worksheet that does not include column headings, the position and the type of data need to match the field order and data types in the destination table. When column headings are present, the name and data type for each column must match the corresponding fields (although the order of the columns and fields do not have to match). Also, check whether the source data contains any fields not included in the table. If the source data does contain other fields, you should add these fields to the destination table or specify to skip them for the import process. The destination table can include fields that are not defined in the source data, provided those fields have their Required property set to No and the fields do not contain any validation rules that prohibit null values.

The source data must include data that is compatible with the table's primary key, and the data in that column must be unique. You receive an import error message if a primary key value in the source data matches one already defined in the destination table. Also, if the Indexed property of any field in the destination table is set to Yes (No Duplicates), the source data must include unique values for that field.

To append records to a table in the current database

1. On the **External Data** tab, in the **Import & Link** group, click **New Data Source**, then click one of the following data sources:

   - **From File**, and then **Excel**

   - **From File**, and then **HTML Document**

   - **From File**, and then **Text File**

   - **From Other Sources**, and then **Outlook Folder**

   IMPORTANT You can append records to a table only from Excel workbooks, text files, HTML documents, and Outlook folders.

   ---

2. In the **Get External Data** dialog box, do the following:

   Click **Browse** to open the **File Open** dialog box. Locate and select the source file, then click **Open**.

   Click **Append A Copy Of The Records To The Table**, and then in the adjacent list, select the table you want to append records to.

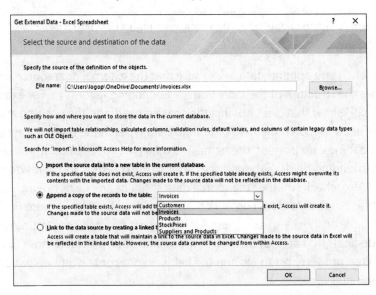

Select a table to append data.

   Click **OK**.

3. Follow the steps in the import wizard (if Access provides one) to import and append the data.

4. In the **Get External Data** dialog box, do the following:

If you want to save the steps of the operation for reuse, select the **Save Import Steps** check box and provide a name and optional description for the steps.

Click **Close**.

Create linked tables from external sources

With linked tables, you can include in your database information that's stored in an external data source. You can create a linked table that's based on an Excel worksheet, a text file, or one of the other external data formats that Access supports. Linking to an Excel worksheet or a text file, for example, creates a one-way link. You can read the data in Access, but you cannot insert or update records—the data is maintained only in the external data source. However, you can link to tables in another Access database and work with those tables in many of the same ways you work with tables in your database. You can add and update records in a table linked to another Access database, but you can't change the table's design. To modify the design, open the table in the source database.

Access adds an entry for a linked table to the Navigation Pane, displaying an icon that identifies the type of data source. The icon includes a small arrow to indicate that the table is a linked table.

Linked tables are identified in the Navigation Pane.

When you link to an Excel worksheet or a text file to create a table, Access provides a wizard (the Link Text Wizard, for example) that functions much like the wizards you follow to import data into a new table.

Tip You can link to tables in other Access databases to work around the restriction on the size of a single Access database file (approximately 2 GB).

If you link to an Access database or to another external data source that is protected with a password, you must provide the password to link successfully. Access can save the password so that you don't need to provide it each time you open the external table. Because Access saves this information, you might want to encrypt your database.

If a source file you have linked to is moved to a different location, you can update the link by using the Linked Table Manager dialog box, which lists each table linked to in the current database.

To link to a table in another Access database

1. On the **External Data** tab, in the **Import & Link** group, click **New Data Source**, click **From Database**, and then click **Access**.

2. In the **Get External Data – Access Database** dialog box, do the following:

   Click **Browse** to open the **File Open** dialog box. Locate and select the source database, then click **Open**.

   Click **Link To The Data Source By Creating A Linked Table**.

   Click **OK** to open the **Link Tables** dialog box.

3. In the **Link Tables** dialog box, select the table or tables you want to link to, then click **OK**.

To link to a text file

1. On the **External Data** tab, in the **Import & Link** group, click **New Data Source**, click **From File**, and then click **Text File**.

2. In the **Get External Data – Text File** dialog box, do the following:

   Click **Browse** to open the **File Open** dialog box. Locate and select the source file, then click **Open**.

   Click **Link To The Data Source By Creating A Linked Table**.

   Click **OK** to start the **Link Text Wizard**.

3. In the **Link Text Wizard**, do the following:

   On the wizard's first page, specify the format of the text file (**Delimited** or **Fixed Width**), then click **Next**.

   Choose the delimiting character or specify column breaks (depending on the format).

   Select **First Row Contains Field Names** if this option applies.

   Click **Next** to work through the remaining pages to set field options.

   Enter a name for the linked table, then click **Finish**.

4. In the **Link Text Wizard** message box that confirms the table was linked, click **OK**.

To link to an Excel worksheet or named range

1. On the **External Data** tab, in the **Import & Link** group, click **New Data Source**, click **From File**, and then click **Excel**.

2. In the **Get External Data – Excel Spreadsheet** dialog box, do the following:

   Click **Browse** to open the **File Open** dialog box. Locate and select the source workbook, then click **Open**.

   Click **Link To The Data Source By Creating A Linked Table**.

   Click **OK** to start the **Link Spreadsheet Wizard**.

3. In the **Link Spreadsheet Wizard**, do the following:

   On the wizard's first page, select the worksheet or named range that contains the data you want to link to, then click **Next**.

   Specify whether the first row of the data includes column headings, then click **Next**.

   Enter a name for the linked table, then click **Finish**.

4. In the **Link Spreadsheet Wizard** message box that confirms the table was linked, click **OK**.

To manage linked tables

1. On the **External Data** tab, in the **Import & Link** group, click **Linked Table Manager**.

2. In the **Linked Table Manager** dialog box, select the check box for the table or tables whose links you want to update, then click **OK**.

3. If the source file is not in the original location, Access opens the **Select New Location** dialog box. In this dialog box, navigate to the new location for the file, select the file, and then click **Open**.

4. In the **Linked Table Manager** message box, click **OK**.

Import tables from other databases

You can import tables from other database files or database management systems. In this section, you learn how to import one or more tables from three common types of databases:

- **SQL Server** This robust and powerful server-based database management system is designed to handle massive amounts of data. To access a SQL Server instance, you need to know the login ID and password to connect to the SQL Server data source.

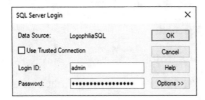

You must log in to access an SQL Server database.

- **Azure Database** This online database management system runs inside an Azure instance in Microsoft's cloud.

- **dBASE** This is a DBF file that you import from a local or network location.

See Also For information on importing tables (as well as other objects) from an Access database, see "Import objects or data from other sources" in Objective 1.1: Modify database structure."

To import one or more tables from an SQL Server database

1. On the **External Data** tab, in the **Import & Link** group, click **New Data Source**, click **From Database**, and then click **From SQL Server**.

2. In the **Get External Data – ODBC Database** dialog box, click **Import The Source Data Into A New Table In The Current Database**, then click **OK**. Access opens the **Select Data Source** dialog box.

    Exam Strategy It is assumed here and on the Access Expert exam that a data source for the SQL Server database has already been created by an administrator and that you have been given the login credentials for the SQL Server.

3. On the **Machine Data Source** tab, click the SQL Server data source, then click **OK**. The **SQL Server Login** dialog box appears.

4. Type the login ID and password required to log in to the SQL Server, then click **OK**. Access displays the **Import Objects** dialog box.

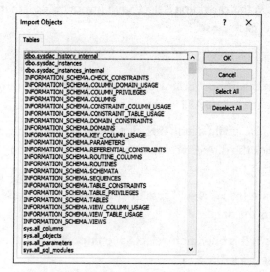

Use the Import Objects dialog box to select the table or tables you want to import.

5. In the **Tables** list, click each table you want to import, and click **OK**. Access imports the data and returns you to the **Get External Data – ODBC Database** dialog box.

6. If you want to save the steps in this operation, select **Save Import Steps**, then click **Save Import**; otherwise, click **Close**.

2

To import one or more tables from an Azure database

1. On the **External Data** tab, in the **Import & Link** group, click **New Data Source**, click **From Database**, and then click **From Azure Database**.

2. In the **Get External Data – ODBC Database** dialog box, click **Import The Source Data Into A New Table In The Current Database**, then click OK. Access opens the **Select Data Source** dialog box.

3. On the **Machine Data Source** tab, click the Azure database data source, then click **OK**. Access prompts you to log in to the database.

4. Type the login ID and password required to log in to the Azure database, then click **OK**. Access displays the **Import Objects** dialog box.

5. In the **Tables** list, click each table you want to import, then click **OK**. Access imports the data and returns you to the **Get External Data – ODBC Database** dialog box.

6. If you want to save the steps in this operation, select **Save Import Steps**, then click **Save Import**; otherwise, click **Close**.

To import a table from a dBASE file

1. On the **External Data** tab, in the **Import & Link** group, click **New Data Source**, click **From Database**, and then click **dBASE File**.

2. In the **Get External Data – dBASE File** dialog box, click **Browse** to display the **File Open** dialog box, click the dBASE file you want to import, and then click **Open**.

3. Click **Import The Source Data Into A New Table In The Current Database**, then click **OK**. Access imports the data.

4. If you want to save the steps in this operation, select **Save Import Steps**, then click **Save Import**; otherwise, click **Close**.

Objective 2.1 practice tasks

The practice files for these tasks are located in the **MOSAccessExpert2019\ Objective2** practice file folder. The folder also contains a result file that you can use to check your work.

➤ In the **AccessExpert_2-1** database, do the following:

❑ If the Info bar appears, click the *Enable Content* button.

❑ Import the **Customers Table** worksheet from the **AccessExpert_2-1** workbook (.xlsx) located in the practice file folder to create a new table in the database, using the worksheet's column headings. Skip importing the Fax field. Use the CustomerID field as the primary key. Name the table *Customers*.

❑ Import the table from the **AccessExpert_2-1** HTML document (.html) located in the practice file folder to create a new table in the database, using the table's column headings. Let Access create the primary key. Name the table *Products*.

❑ Import the structure and data of the Suppliers table from the **AccessExpert_2-1** XML document (.xml) located in the practice file folder to create a new table in the database.

❑ Import the **AccessExpert_2-1** text file (.csv) located in the practice file folder and append the data to the existing Orders table in the database. Import the text as a comma-delimited file using the text file's column headings. Use the OrderID field as the primary key.

❑ Import the **AccessExpert_2-1** text file (.txt) located in the practice file folder to create a linked table in the database. Import the text as a fixed-width file using the text file's column headings. Name the first field *Currency*, the second field *Per $US*, and the third field *To $US*. Name the table *Exchange Rates*.

❑ Open the **AccessExpert_2-1** text file (.txt) located in the practice file folder. In the second column of the Argentine Peso record, change the value 8.77 to **8.57**. Save and close the text file, then update the Exchange Rates table to incorporate the changed value.

❑ Open the **AccessExpert_2-1_results** database. Compare the two databases to check your work. Then close the open databases.

Objective 2.2: Manage tables

This topic covers various aspects of managing tables. Managing a table involves activities such as hiding or freezing fields to make a large datasheet easier to view, adding a Total row to display summary values for fields (a count of how many orders are recorded, for example, or the total sum or average amount of payments you've received), and adding descriptive text to table fields.

Hide fields in tables

When a table includes either a relatively large number of fields or several fields that contain relatively long entries, when you open the table in Datasheet view you might not be able to see all the fields on your screen. This means that you have to scroll horizontally to view the fields you can't see. To avoid scrolling to view a field, you can hide fields you don't need to refer to (the primary key field, for example, which you would very rarely change). You can also freeze fields so that a specific field (or fields) remains in view as you scroll.

You can freeze a field whose column is at any position in the datasheet. Access moves the column or columns you freeze to the far left of the datasheet, placing the column or columns before any others. Unfreezing the field does not return this column (or columns) to its original position in the table. You need to drag the column heading to place the column where you want it in the table.

You can select more than one field to hide or freeze, but the fields must be adjoining fields in the datasheet. Access selects the first field you select and each field to the left or right of the next field you select.

To hide fields in a table

1. Open the table in Datasheet view.

2. Do either of the following:

   - To hide one field, right-click the field column heading, then click **Hide Fields**.
   - To hide multiple adjacent fields, click the first field column heading, press and hold the **Shift** key, and click the last field column heading. Then right-click the selection and click **Hide Fields**.

To show hidden fields in a table

1. Open the table in Datasheet view.

2. Right-click a column heading, then click **Unhide Fields**.

3. In the **Unhide Columns** dialog box, select the check boxes for the fields you want to show.

4. Click **Close**.

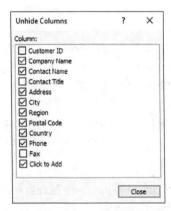

Unhide fields by selecting them in this dialog box.

To freeze fields in a table

1. Open the table in Datasheet view.

2. Do either of the following:

   - To freeze one field, right-click the field column heading, then click **Freeze Fields**.

   - To freeze multiple adjacent fields, click the first field column heading, press and hold the Shift key, and click the last field column heading. Then right-click the selection and click **Freeze Fields**.

To unfreeze fields in a table

→ In Datasheet view, right-click a column heading, then click **Unfreeze All Fields**.

Add Total rows

As you will learn in Objective group 3, "Create and modify queries," one use of a query is to summarize data—that is, to count how many orders were placed in a month, for example, or to calculate the aggregate value of a number or currency field. You can also summarize data in a table by adding a Total row to display summary values for one or more fields. A Total row uses built-in functions such as Sum and Count. For Sum to be applied to a field, the field's data type must be set to Number or Currency. For fields that don't use a numeric data type (such as a text field), you can apply the Count function. In numeric fields, you can also apply the functions Average, Maximum, Minimum, Standard Deviation, and Variance.

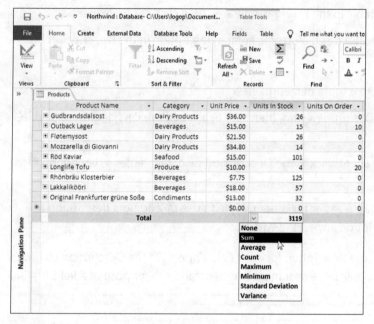

Total rows show calculated totals.

To add and configure a Total row for a table

1. Open the table in Datasheet view.

2. On the **Home** tab, in the **Records** group, click **Totals**. Access adds a **Total** row to the bottom of the table.

3. For each column in the **Total** row where you want a total to appear, click in the column, click the arrow that appears on the left side of the cell, and then select the function you want to apply.

To remove the Total row from a table

→ On the **Home** tab, in the **Records** group, click **Totals**.

Add table descriptions

One of the properties you can define for a table is *Description*. Adding a description is another step you can take to document the objects and logic in your database. You can add a description in Design view by displaying the table's property sheet or in a table's Properties dialog box.

To add a description to a table from the Navigation Pane

1. Right-click the table in the **Navigation Pane**, then click **Table Properties**.

2. In the table's **Properties** dialog box, enter a description in the **Description** box, then click **OK**.

To add a description to a table in Design view

1. Right-click the Design view grid, then click **Properties**. Access displays the table's property sheet.

2. In the property sheet, click in the **Description** field, then enter a description for the table.

You can also make a table easier for other people to use by adding a description to each field. That description appears in two places:

- In Design view, the description for each field appears in the Description column, which enables other table designers to understand the purpose of a field.

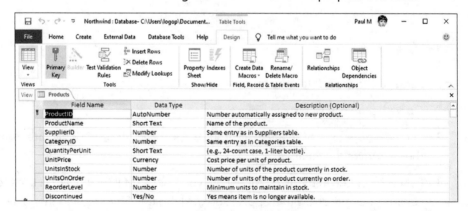

In Design view, field descriptions appear in the Description column.

- In Datasheet view, the description for a field appears in the Access status bar when the user navigates to that field. This helps table users to understand the data.

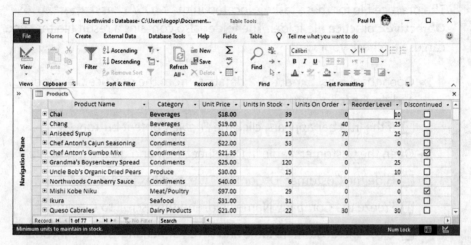

In Datasheet view, a field's description appears in the status bar when the field is active.

See Also You can also change the default field names to captions that are easier for users to read and understand. To learn how to do this, see "To change a field caption" in "Objective 2.4: Create and modify fields."

To add descriptions to a table's fields

1. Right-click the table you want to modify, then click **Design View**.

2. For each field, use the **Description** column to enter descriptive text for the field.

   IMPORTANT Your descriptions should be as clear and as accurate as possible, but they should also be succinct since each description is limited to 255 characters.

Objective 2.2 practice tasks

The practice file for these tasks is located in the **MOSAccessExpert2016\ Objective2** practice file folder. The folder also contains a result file that you can use to check your work.

➤ Open the **AccessExpert_2-2** database from the practice file folder and do the following:

  ❑ If the Info bar appears, click the *Enable Content* button.

➤ Open the Customers table in Datasheet view and do the following:

  ❑ Hide the Customer ID, Contact Title, and Fax fields.

  ❑ Freeze the Company Name field, and then scroll to the right.

  ❑ Close the Customers table and save your changes to the layout.

➤ Open the Products table in Datasheet view and do the following:

  ❑ Add a Total row to the Products table.

  ❑ In the Total row, set the Units In Stock field to display the total units that are available.

  ❑ In the Total row, set the Units On Order field to display the total units that have been ordered.

  ❑ In the Total row, set the Discontinued field to display the number of items that have been discontinued.

➤ Close the Products table, then do the following:

  ❑ Add the description *Our loyal customers* to the Customers table.

  ❑ Open the Customers table in Design view and add the description *Unique Five-Character Code Based On The Company Name* to the Customer ID field.

➤ Open the **AccessExpert_2-2_results** database. Compare the two databases to check your work. Then close the open databases.

Objective 2.3: Manage table records

Over time, a database can grow to include thousands of records. Locating a specific record by scrolling through a table's datasheet (or by using a form) is inefficient in circumstances like this. To locate a record or a group of records that share specific criteria, you can use commands to find, replace, sort, and filter records in Datasheet view.

Find and replace data

Find And Replace is a single feature with two parts: one that enables you to locate text and another that enables you to replace found text with other text. Both features can save you tremendous amounts of time, particularly in large tables.

In the Find And Replace dialog box, you use the Find tab to locate text within records. You can search for numbers, partial words, entire words, or phrases. You use the Replace tab to also locate text within a table, except you can also replace the found text with some other text that you specify.

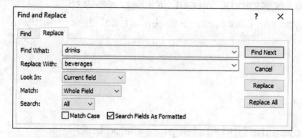

Use the Find And Replace dialog box to locate, and optionally replace, text within an Access table.

After you enter the value you're looking for in the Find What box, you can refine the search as follows:

- Use the **Look In** list to specify whether Access should search the current field or the entire table (the **Current Document** option).

- Use any of the following three options in the **Match** list:
  - **Whole Field** Use this option (the default setting) to find records with values that match the entire text string you enter in the **Find What** box. For example, if you enter **Blue**, Access does not find records whose value is Light Blue, Dark Blue, or Navy Blue.

- **Any Part Of Field** Use this option if you want to locate records that contain the text string you enter in any part of the field. If you enter **Blue** with this option selected, Access finds records for Blue, Light Blue, Dark Blue, and Navy Blue (and those like them).

- **Start Of Field** Use this option to locate records that begin with a specific string of characters—all records whose **Description** field starts with *Spa*, for example, to find the records for *Spanish olive oil*, *Spaghetti*, *Sparkling water*, and *Spanakopita*.

- Use the **Search** list to specify whether Access should search down, up, or all (both directions).

- Select the **Match Case** option to implement a case-sensitive search.

- Select the **Search Fields As Formatted** option to search a field that has a particular format or an input mask. With this option selected, Access searches the data as it is displayed instead of how Access stores it. This option is particularly useful in date and time fields.

Use the options on the Replace tab in the Find And Replace dialog box when you want to insert new data for the data Access finds. You can click Replace All to replace all instances of the data, or you can click Replace to replace just the currently highlighted instance.

To find table data

1. Open the table in Datasheet view.

2. Do either of the following to open the **Find And Replace** dialog box:

   - On the **Home** tab, in the **Find** group, click **Find**.

   - Press **Ctrl+F**.

3. In the **Find And Replace** dialog box, on the **Find** tab, enter the text you want to locate in the **Find What** box.

4. In the **Look In** list, select **Current Field** or **Current Document** (which refers to the entire table).

5. In the **Match** list, select **Whole Field**, **Any Part Of Field**, or **Start Of Field**.

6. In the **Search** list, select **All**, **Up**, or **Down**.

7. Select the **Match Case** check box if you want to perform a case-sensitive search.

8. Select the **Search Fields As Formatted** check box if you want to search the data as it is formatted in the datasheet.

9. Click **Find Next**. Access highlights the next instance of the text you typed in the **Find What** text box.

10. Repeat step 9 to find more instances of the text. When you have run through the entire table, Access displays a message box telling you it has finished searching the records.

11. Click **OK**, then click **Cancel** to close the **Find And Replace** dialog box.

To replace table data

1. Open the table in Datasheet view.

2. Do either of the following to open the **Find And Replace** dialog box:
   - On the **Home** tab, in the **Find** group, click **Find**.
   - Press **Ctrl+F**.

3. On the **Replace** tab, enter the text you want to find in the **Find What** box.

4. Use the **Replace With** text box to enter the text you want to substitute for the found text.

5. In the **Look In** list, select **Current Field** or **Current Document** (which refers to the entire table).

6. In the **Match** list, select **Whole Field**, **Any Part Of Field**, or **Start Of Field**.

7. In the **Search** list, select **All**, **Up**, or **Down**.

8. Select the **Match Case** check box if you want to perform a case-sensitive search.

9. Select the **Search Fields As Formatted** check box if you want to search the data as it is formatted in the datasheet.

10. Click **Find Next** until you come across the next instance of the text you want to replace.

11. Replace the text:

- If you want to replace the text one instance at a time, click **Replace**. Access makes the replacement and then highlights the next instance of the text. If you don't want to replace this instance, click **Find Next** until you locate the next replacement; otherwise, keep clicking **Replace**.

- If you want to replace all instances of the text, click **Replace All**. If Access displays a warning that you will not be able to undo the Replace operation, click **Yes** to confirm that you want to continue.

12. When you have run through the entire table or all instances of the text, Access displays a message box telling you it has finished replacing or searching the records.

13. Click **OK**, then click **Cancel** to close the **Find And Replace** dialog box.

Sort records

By sorting the records in a table, you can arrange a datasheet in an order in which you can more easily find a specific record (such as the name of a contact) or a set of related records (for example, all orders shipped on September 12). You can sort a field in two ways:

- **Ascending** Sorts the field in ascending order, as follows: alphabetical (A to Z) for text fields; smallest to largest (0 to 9) for numeric fields; oldest to newest for date and time fields.

- **Descending** Sorts the field in descending order, as follows: reverse alphabetical (Z to A) for text fields; largest to smallest for numeric fields; newest to oldest for date and time fields.

You can also sort a table by multiple columns. For example, you can sort a table on the Launch Date field in ascending order (January through December) and the Campaign Budget field in descending order (largest to smallest) to see the sequence of larger expenditures for campaigns scheduled to launch over a period of time. When you sort by multiple fields, apply the second, or *inner*, sort first (in this case, budgets in descending order).

Text fields provide the sorting options Sort A To Z or Sort Z To A. Number fields have the commands Sort Smallest To Largest or Sort Largest To Smallest, and date fields use Sort Oldest To Newest and Sort Newest To Oldest.

For more advanced sorts, Access displays a window with a list of the table's fields in the top pane and a grid in the bottom pane. (If you open this window when a sort order is applied, the grid shows the field and sort criteria specified.)

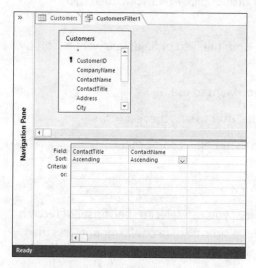

Sort by multiple fields by adding them to the grid.

To sort by a field, you add it to the Field row in the grid. By adding other fields to the Field row, you can create a multiple-field sort. The Sort row provides the Ascending and Descending options, which you use to apply a sort order.

To sort records from the Home tab

1. Open the table in Datasheet view.

2. Click the field you want to sort by.

3. On the **Home** tab, in the **Sort & Filter** group, click **Ascending** or **Descending**.

To sort records by using a shortcut menu

1. Open the table in Datasheet view.

2. Right-click the field you want to sort by, then click the command for the sort order you want to use. (The command names depend on the field's data type.)

To set up and apply an advanced sort

1. Open the table in Datasheet view.

2. On the **Home** tab, in the **Sort & Filter** group, click **Advanced**, then click **Advanced Filter/Sort**.

3. In the **Advanced Filter/Sort** window, drag the field or fields you want to sort by to the **Field** row in the grid.

4. In the **Sort** row, select the sort order you want to use.

5. In the **Sort & Filter** group, click **Toggle Filter** to sort the records.

6. Click **Remove Sort** to return the table to its default sort order.

Filter records

By applying a filter to a table in Datasheet view, you can select a specific set of records to review, such as all orders placed on or after a specific date or all amounts less than or greater than the target you specify.

Access provides several ways to filter records. You can filter by one or more of the values in a field, for example. Another way is to filter by selection, using either the entire value or a portion of it as the filter criterion. After selecting the criterion, you can apply an expression to apply the filter. For text fields, you can apply the expressions Equals *Value*, Does Not Equal *Value*, and Contains *Value*. For date fields, the expressions include Equals *Date*, Does Not Equal *Date*, On Or Before *Date*, On Or After *Date*, and Between, which lets you specify a date range to use as the filter. For Number fields, Less Than Or Equal To and Greater Than Or Equal To options are included along with Equals, Does Not Equal, and Between.

You can filter by selection progressively to home in on a specific set of records. For example, the first time you apply a filter, the criteria you use might reduce 200 records to 75. Filter the remaining records by using different criteria to review a smaller subset.

Access provides additional filters based on a field's data type. The Text Filters command displays the Equals, Does Not Equal, Begins With, Does Not Begin With,

Contains, Does Not Contain, Ends With, and Does Not End With filters. You choose a filter, then specify the criteria in the Custom Filter dialog box that Access displays.

The Date Filters commands include options such as Before, After, and Between, in addition to Next Week, Last Week, Year To Date, and many others. You can also choose All Dates In Period and then choose a period such as Quarter 1 or a specific month of the year.

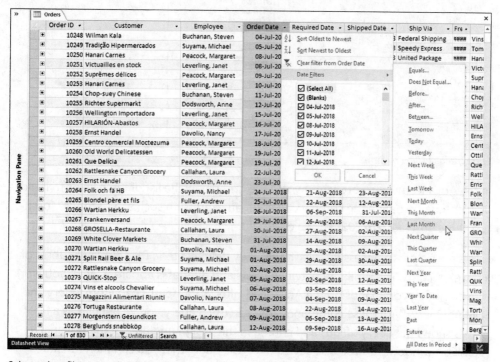

Select a date filter to apply it to the field.

Advanced filtering options include Filter By Form and Advanced Filter/Sort. When you filter by form, Access opens a blank datasheet with the names of the table's fields at the top of each column. You can then enter or select criteria for the field you want to use in the filter. You can choose a value for more than one field to create an AND condition—for example, a filter that displays records for products whose size equals Large *and* whose color equals Blue. Use the Or tab at the bottom of the window to set up additional values for the filter. If you specify filter criteria on the Or tab, Access returns records that match the criteria specified on either the Look For tab or the Or tab.

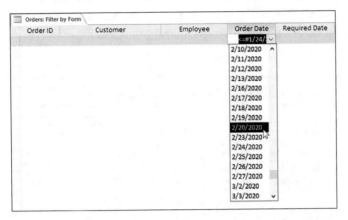

Select criteria to filter by form.

In the Advanced Filter/Sort window, use the grid below the list of table fields to build filter criteria. To define the criteria, you enter an expression such as *= "France"* for a text value or *<=#2/20/2020#* for a date field.

Filters are similar to Access queries in that they define criteria that display a subset of a table's records. The similarity between filters and queries is apparent when you work with two other commands on the Advanced Filter/Sort menu: Load From Query and Save As Query. With these commands, you can use a query you've defined as a filter. Access shows the query's fields and criteria in the design grid area of the Advanced Filter/Sort window. You can also save a filter as a query that you can then run independently or include in other queries.

Tip Use the Clear Grid command on the Advanced Filter Options menu to remove any criteria from the grid.

To filter by a field in Datasheet view

1. Do either of the following to display the **Sort & Filter** menu for the field you want to filter by:

   - Select the field you want to filter by, and then on the **Home** tab, in the **Sort & Filter** group, click **Filter**.

   - In the field header of the field you want to filter by, click the arrow.

2. On the **Sort & Filter** menu, clear the **(Select All)** check box.

3. Select the check box for each field value you want to view.

4. Click **OK** to apply the filter.

To filter by selection in Datasheet view

1. Select the value or the portion of a value you want to use as the filter.

2. On the **Home** tab, in the **Sort & Filter** group, click the **Selection** button, then click *operator value*, where *operator* is a conditional operator such as Equals, Does Not Equal, Contains (for text), or Less Than Or Equal To (for numbers), and *value* is the value you selected in step 1. (Clicking **Toggle Filter** removes the filter from the table.)

To filter by form

1. On the **Home** tab, in the **Sort & Filter** group, click **Advanced**, then click **Filter By Form**.

2. In the **Filter By Form** window, on the **Look For** tab, enter the value in the field or fields you want to use as the filter.

3. Click the **Or** tab to set up alternative conditions.

4. In the **Sort & Filter** group, click **Toggle Filter** to apply the filter. (Clicking **Toggle Filter** again removes the filter.)

To create an advanced filter

1. On the **Home** tab, in the **Sort & Filter** group, click **Advanced,** then click **Advanced Filter/Sort**.

2. In the **Advanced Filter/Sort** window, in the **Field** row in the grid, select the fields you want to use in the filter.

3. In the **Criteria** row, specify the expression to use in the filter.

4. In the **Sort & Filter** group, click **Toggle Filter** to apply the filter. (Clicking **Toggle Filter** again removes the filter.)

To use a query as a filter

1. On the **Home** tab, in the **Sort & Filter** group, click **Advanced**, then click **Advanced Filter/Sort**.

2. Click **Advanced** again, then choose **Load From Query**.

3. In the **Applicable Filter** dialog box, select the query you want to use as a filter, then click **OK**.

4. In the **Sort & Filter** group, click **Toggle Filter** to apply the filter. (Clicking **Toggle Filter** again removes the filter.)

To save a filter as a query

1. On the **Home** tab, in the **Sort & Filter** group, click **Advanced**, then click **Advanced Filter/Sort**.

2. In the **Advanced Filter/Sort** window, in the **Field** row in the grid, select the fields you want to use in the filter.

3. In the **Criteria** row, specify the expression to use in the filter.

4. Click **Advanced**, then choose **Save As Query**.

5. Enter a name for the query in the **Save As Query** dialog box, then click **OK**.

Objective 2.3 practice tasks

The practice files for these tasks are located in the **MOSAccessExpert2019\ Objective2** practice file folder. The folder also contains a result file that you can use to check your work.

➤ Open the **AccessExpert_2-3** database from the practice file folder and do the following:

❑ Open the Customers table in Datasheet view.

❑ In the Contact Title field, replace all instances of *Marketing Assistant* with *Marketing Specialist*.

❑ Sort the table records in ascending order by the Country field and then by the Company Name field.

❑ Open the Orders table in Datasheet view.

❑ Filter the table to show only records where the Employee field is *Peacock, Margaret*.

❑ Open the Products table in Datasheet view.

❑ Create an advanced filter that shows only records that have a category of *Confections* and a unit price greater than or equal to $30. Apply the filter, then save the filter as a query with the name *ExpensiveConfections*.

➤ Open the **AccessExpert_2-3_results** database. Compare the two databases to check your work. Then close the open databases.

Objective 2.4: Create and modify fields

Table fields are defined not only by their name and data type. *Field properties* add to the definition of a field by specifying a format (as for Date/Time fields), whether a field is required, whether Access creates an index for that field, the field's default value, and other information.

This topic expands on how tables are defined. It describes how you create and delete fields and how you work with field properties to fine-tune a table's design. You learn how to set field sizes and captions, input masks, field validation rules, and default values. This section also describes how to increment the value in a field automatically and how to change a field's data type.

You can accomplish most of the tasks described in this section with the table open in either Design view or Datasheet view.

Add and delete fields

In Design view, you can add a field by entering the field name in the first blank row or insert a row where you want the field to appear. (In the latter case, the row is inserted above the row you select.) If you delete a field that contains data, Access asks for confirmation, warning that you will permanently delete the field and its data.

When a table is open in Datasheet view, you add and delete fields in a couple of ways. The Click To Add column heading displays a list of field data types you can apply to the field. You can also add fields by working with commands in the Add & Delete group on the Table Tools Fields tool tab. A field you insert appears to the right of the field selected in the table. The Add & Delete group provides options that correspond to Access data types. Use the Short Text, Number, Currency, Date/Time, and Yes/No commands to insert a field and apply that data type. (The Number command inserts a field whose Field Size property is set to Long Integer.) The More Fields command opens a menu that provides additional data types, including Attachment, Hyperlink, and Long Text, plus a variety of formats for the Number, Date/Time, and Yes/No data types.

The last category in the More Fields list is the Quick Start group. These Quick Start items contain one or more fields that are assigned appropriate data types. You can add Quick Start items (also known as *data type application parts*) to a table to define a group of related fields.

In fields provided by Quick Start data types, many field properties are set so that you can start using the fields to capture data without additional work. For example, the Address item adds fields named Address, City, State Province, ZIP Postal, and Country Region. (You can rename the fields to fit your database.) The Payment Type item inserts a lookup field that includes the list Cash, Credit Card, Check, and In-Kind.

You can also create your own Quick Start data types. Data type application parts that you create are stored in the default location for Access database templates (usually AppData\Roaming\Microsoft\Templates under your user profile) and use the .accft filename extension. You can share these files so that colleagues and coworkers can also work with the data types you create.

The Add & Delete group also includes a Delete button. Keep in mind that Access prevents you from deleting a field that is part of a relationship and displays a message box informing you that you must delete the relationship first.

To insert a field in an existing table in Design view

➜ Right-click the existing field above which you want to insert the new field, then click **Insert Rows**.

To add a field to a table in Design view

1. Using either a blank row that you've inserted in the table, or the first blank row below the table's existing fields, use the **Field Name** column to enter the name of the field.

2. In the **Data Type** column, select the data type for the field.

3. In the **Description** column, enter a brief description of the field.

4. In the **Field Properties** area, set properties such as **Field Size**, **Format**, **Indexed**, and **Required**.

To add a field to a table in Datasheet view

1. To the right of the last field, click the **Click To Add** arrow, then select the data type you want to apply to the field.

2. Replace the **Field***N* column heading with the name of the field.

Or

1. Select the field that you want to insert the new field after.

2. On the **Fields** tool tab, in the **Add & Delete** group, click the data type for the field you want to insert. Click **More Fields** to display an extended list of data types.

3. In the column heading row, replace the placeholder name (**Field***N*) with the name of the field.

To insert a Quick Start data type in Datasheet view

1. Select the field that you want to insert the new fields after.

2. On the **Fields** tool tab, in the **Add & Delete** group, click **More Fields**, and in the **Quick Start** section of the menu, click the field or field set you want to insert.

To define a custom data type application part

1. In the datasheet, select the field or fields you want to include in the custom data type.

2. On the **Fields** tool tab, in the **Add & Delete** group, click **More Fields**, then click **Save Selection As New Data Type**.

3. In the **Create New Data Type from Fields** dialog box, enter a name and description for the custom data type. Select an entry in the **Category** list, or enter the name for a new category. Then click **OK**.

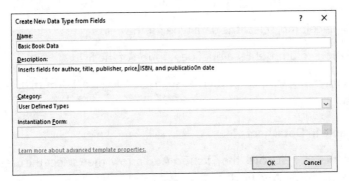

Save a set of fields as a data type application part.

To rename a field in Datasheet view

1. Right-click the field heading, then click **Rename Field** to activate the field name for editing.

2. Enter the new field name, then press **Enter**.

To delete a field in Datasheet view

1. Right-click the field heading, then click **Delete Field**.

2. When Access prompts you to confirm that you want to delete the field, click **Yes**.

To rename a field in Design view

➜ In the **Field Name** column, select the field name, then enter the new name.

To delete a field in Design view

1. Right-click the row selector to the left of the field name, then click **Delete Row**.

2. When Access prompts you to confirm that you want to delete the field, click **Yes**.

Add validation rules to fields

The data type you assign to a field prevents some erroneous data entry. For example, enter the text **"*test*"** in a Date/Time field, and Access displays a warning telling you that the value does not match the Date/Time data type. You can define a validation rule for a field to further control the data a user can enter. Validation rules don't apply for all types of fields. You use them most often for fields that use the Short Text, Number, Currency, or Date/Time data types.

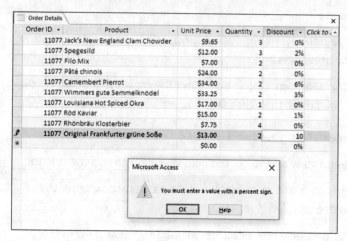

Using a validation rule and message.

A simple validation rule might compare the value of a field to one or more constants. For example, enter the expression **<*1000*** as a field validation rule to ensure that the field contains no values greater than or equal to 1,000. Be sure to enclose text strings in quotation marks, and enclose dates with pound signs (#). For example, you can create a validation rule that specifies a list of valid values for a product size field by using the expression *"Large" OR "Medium" OR "Small"*. For a Date/Time field, the expression *BETWEEN #1/1/2020#* and *#12/31/2020#* sets the field validation rule so that only dates in calendar year 2020 are valid.

You can use the LIKE operator and wildcard characters to specify a valid pattern. For example, for a five-digit US ZIP Code, use the expression *LIKE "#####"*. You can also define an error message that Access displays when invalid data is entered in the field.

To add a field validation rule in Datasheet view

1. Open the table in Datasheet view and select the field you want to add the rule to.

2. On the **Fields** tool tab, in the **Field Validation** group, click the **Validation** arrow, then click **Field Validation Rule**.

3. In the **Expression Builder**, enter the expression that defines the rule, then click **OK**.

To create a validation message

1. On the **Fields** tool tab, in the **Field Validation** group, click the **Validation** arrow, then click **Field Validation Message**.

2. In the **Enter Validation Message** dialog box, enter the message that Access displays if users enter invalid data, then click **OK**.

To add a field validation rule in Design view

1. Open the table in Design view and select the field you want to add the rule to.

2. In the **Field Properties** area, in the **Validation Rule** property box, enter the expression for the validation rule.

3. In the **Validation Text** property box, enter the message you want Access to display if users enter invalid data.

Modify field properties

By default, a field's name identifies the field in the column heading in Datasheet view or when the field is added to a form or a report. You can enter a caption to change the display name for the field. For example, a database designer might name fields by using internal capitalization, such as *TaskName*. To make the field's name more readable on forms and reports, enter **Task Name** as the field's caption.

The Field Size property for a field that uses the Short Text data type specifies the maximum number of characters that can be entered in the field. For example, suppose your company uses a six-character product code, with a combination of letters and numbers. You could set the Field Size property to **6** to ensure that no user enters more characters than are allowed.

For a Number field, the Field Size property specifies the extent of the numbers the field can contain (for example, Byte, Long Integer, and Single).

By using the Default Value command in Datasheet view (or the Default Value property box in Design view), you define the value that Access enters automatically for a field. For example, you might use the built-in function *Now()* in an order date field to fill in today's date when a new order is entered. You can also use a text or numerical constant as a field's default value. For example, you could set a default value for a country/region field so that the field is set automatically to the value you use most often. Likewise, if you sold certain products only with a minimum order quantity (only in units of 12, for example), you could set the Default Value property in the quantity field to reflect that amount.

When you're building a table, the best approach is to set the data type for a field once and not change it. Changing a field's data type can be problematic, especially after data has been added to a table. For example, if you change the data type for a Date/Time field to a Number field, the dates are converted to their serial value (12/31/2020 becomes 43830). Access can handle the conversion of dates to numbers (and back to dates), but other data types don't work as smoothly. Access displays a warning if you change a field's data type from Long Text to Short Text, telling you that some data will be lost.

To change a field caption

➜ In Datasheet view, on the **Fields** tool tab, in the **Properties** group, click **Name & Caption**.

➜ In Design view, enter the caption in the **Caption** property box.

To change a field size

→ In Datasheet view, to change the field size for a text field, click the **Fields** tool tab, then select the field. In the **Properties** group, enter the field size in the **Field Size** box.

→ In Design view, select the field, and then, in the **Field Properties** area, click in the **Field Size** property box. For a number field, select the field size setting from the list Access provides; for a text field, enter the value you want to use.

To set the default value for a field

→ In Datasheet view, on the **Fields** tool tab, in the **Properties** group, click **Default Value** to open the **Expression Builder**, and then enter the default value or use the **Expression Builder** to create an expression that calculates the default value.

→ In Design view, in the **Field Properties** area, click in the **Default Value** property box, then do either of the following:

- Enter the default value.

- Click the ellipsis button (**...**) in the property box to open the **Expression Builder**, then enter the value or expression there.

To change the data type of a field

→ In Design view, select the new value in the **Data Type** list.

→ In Datasheet view, on the **Fields** tool tab, in the **Formatting** group, expand the **Data Type** list, then click the data type you want.

Automate field values and formatting

Assign the AutoNumber data type to a field to have Access add a unique number in that field as you add records to a table. AutoNumber is often assigned to an ID field that is used as the table's primary key.

A table can include only one AutoNumber field whose Field Size property is set to Long Integer. (You can use the AutoNumber data type for other fields if the Field Size property is set to Replication ID.) In Design view, check the setting for the New Values property for an AutoNumber field. The default setting is Increment, which means Access assigns numbers sequentially. The Random setting produces random numbers for new records. You might use the Random setting to create unique-order IDs.

An input mask defines a specific pattern for the data in a field. Adding an input mask to a field assists users with entering data correctly. Access provides input masks for data such as phone numbers, US Social Security numbers, ZIP Codes, passwords, and date formats. It is important to remember that an input mask does not affect how data is stored. A field's data type and other properties define that format. An input mask affects only whether the data has been entered in a format Access will accept.

The Input Mask Wizard lists the input masks available for the data type of the currently selected field. For a Date/Time field, Access provides entries such as Long Time, Short Date, and Medium Date. For Short Text fields, the list includes input masks for phone numbers, ZIP Codes, and other sorts of data.

Input masks keep data consistent.

You can enter sample data in the Try It box to view how the mask controls data entry. For example, select the Short Date mask, then enter a month abbreviation in the Try It box. You can specify how an input mask is designed by using special characters to define the mask. In a mask, a zero (0) indicates that a user must enter a digit (from 0 through 9) in that placeholder. A nine (9) marks an optional digit. An uppercase L is used to denote a required letter. An optional letter is marked with a question mark (?). You can create an input mask of your own by using the defined special characters to set up the mask.

See Also You can find a complete list of special characters and how to use them in the article "Control data entry formats with input masks" on the Office support site at *https://support.office.com*.

To configure a field to automatically increment the field value

1. Open the table in Design view and select the field you want to automatically increment.

2. Set the field data type to **AutoNumber**.

3. In the **Field Properties** area, expand the **New Values** property list, then click **Increment**.

To specify an input mask for a field

1. Open the table in Design view and select the field you want to apply an input mask to.

2. Click in the **Input Mask** property box, then click the ellipsis to start the **Input Mask Wizard**.

3. Work through the wizard to select the mask you want to use, click **Edit List** to modify a built-in mask, or create one of your own.

Objective 2.4 practice tasks

The practice file for these tasks is located in the **MOSAccessExpert2019\
Objective2** practice file folder. The folder also contains a result file that you
can use to check your work.

➤ Open the **AccessExpert_2-4** database and do the following:

❏ If the Info bar appears, click the *Enable Content* button.

❏ Open the Customers table in Datasheet view.

❏ Select the fields Company Name, Contact Name, and Contact Title,
then create a Quick Start data type named ***Contact Basics***.

❏ Create a new table in Design view. Add a field named *ContactID*.
Set the field to the *AutoNumber* data type and mark this field as the
table's primary key. Save the table and name it ***Contacts***.

❏ Switch to Datasheet view, then add the *Contact Basics* data type
application part to the Contacts table. Save and close the table.

❏ Open the Order Details table in Design view. Create a validation
rule for the Quantity field so that amounts entered must be less
than 100. Enter the validation text ***Order quantities of 100 or
more require approval***.

❏ Save the table, then switch to Datasheet view.

❏ Update the Quantity field in the first record to 101, then click away
from the field. Observe the message Access displays. Click *OK* in the
message box, and then reset the field to its original value.

❏ For the Employees table, use the *Name & Caption* command to
update the *Caption* property for the Courtesy field so that it reads
Title of Courtesy.

❏ Save the table, then switch to Design view.

❑ Change the format of the BirthDate field to *Long Date*.

❑ Create an input mask for the HireDate field that uses the *Medium Date* format.

➤ Open the **AccessExpert_2-4_results** database. Compare the two databases to check your work. Then close the open databases.

Objective group 3

Create and modify queries

The skills tested in this section of the Microsoft Office Specialist Expert exam for Microsoft Access 365 and Microsoft Access 2019 relate to creating and using queries. Specifically, the following objectives are associated with this set of skills:

3.1   Create and run queries

3.2   Modify queries

If you have a large amount of data in a table, you will not usually want or need to work directly with the raw data. Instead, it is better to work with data that has been sorted and filtered in some way, two operations that you can quickly combine by creating a query. Although the name implies that queries are a sort of question, it is more useful to think of them as *requests*. In the simplest case, a *query* is a request to see a particular subset of your data in a particular order. In more complex cases, queries help you manage database records. For example, you can run a query to delete records or to append data to a table.

This chapter guides you in studying ways to create and modify queries, create calculated fields, and group within queries.

To complete the practice tasks in this chapter, you need the practice files contained in the **MOSAccessExpert2019\Objective3** practice file folder. For more information, see "Download the practice files" in this book's Introduction.

Objective 3.1: Create and run queries

You can create a query in Design view or use a wizard to create most or all of the query for you. (Access provides wizards that you use to create different kinds of queries.) In the Query Designer, you add the tables and fields a query requires and define criteria that Access applies to display or act on a specific set of records.

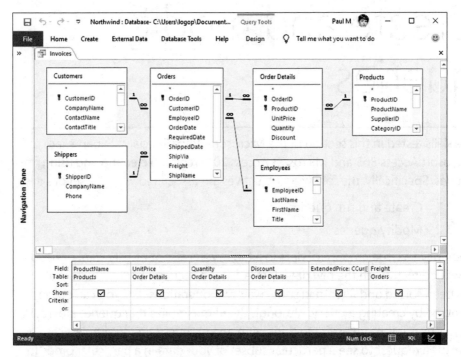

A query based on multiple tables in Design view.

This topic describes how to run a query and how to save and delete a query. You also examine how to create various types of queries, including select queries, crosstab queries, parameter queries, action queries, and queries that use multiple tables.

Run queries

You can run a query directly from the Navigation Pane or by using commands. Running a query displays the query results in Datasheet view, where you can then sort and filter the records, export the query's data, and perform other operations.

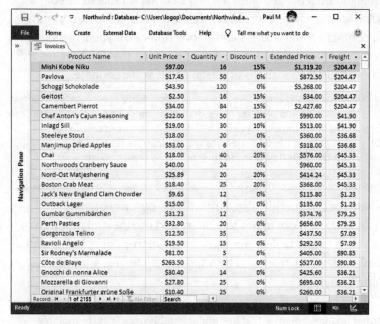

Run a query to see its results in Datasheet view.

When you work in the Query Designer, as you add or remove fields and define criteria and other query properties, you can run the query to view the records that the query returns. You can then return to Design view to make additional modifications to the query and run the query again to check the effects of the changes.

To run a query from the Navigation Pane

→ Double-click the query.

→ Right-click the query, then click **Open**.

To run a query from Design view

1. Open the query in Design view.

2. On the **Design** tool tab, in the **Results** group, click **Run**.

Create select queries

A *select query* returns all or a subset of the records stored in one or more tables. When you create a select query, you specify which fields you want to use, and you can define criteria to return a specific set of records. One simple illustration of a select query is as a record source for a mailing list. For example, by using a contacts table as the basis for the query, you could include name, address, and related fields in the query without adding fields for a contact's email address and phone number. If you're sending a mailing to contacts in specific locations, you could define criteria that limit the records the query returns to contacts in the locations or postal codes you designate.

Exam Strategy   Select queries are the basis of other types of queries described in this chapter, including crosstab queries and action queries. On Exam MO-500, Microsoft Access Expert (Access and Access 2019), you might not need to specifically demonstrate how to create a select query, but you will need the skills described in this section to create other types of queries.

Select queries (and other types of queries) also illustrate one purpose of table relationships. You can add two or more tables to a query and use their relationship to retrieve a set of records from all the tables—for example, all high-priority tasks related to projects for a particular customer, managed by a specific employee, and with a completion date within 30 days.

See Also   For more information about queries that use multiple tables, see "Create multiple-table queries" later in this topic.

To create a select query, you can use the Simple Query Wizard or create the query in the Query Designer. In the Query Designer, you can add criteria to the query. The wizard provides an option that opens the Query Designer if you need it.

The Simple Query Wizard tailors its steps based on factors such as the following:

- If you add fields from only one table and those fields store only text data (not numeric data), the wizard prompts you to name the query and specify whether to open the query to view the records it returns or open the query in Design view for modification.
- If you include numeric or date fields or fields from more than one table, the wizard prompts you to create a detail query or a summary query. A detail query shows each individual record that the query returns. In a summary query, you can total the values in a field or determine the field's average, minimum, or maximum value.

- When date fields are present in a summary query, the wizard also prompts you to choose an option for how you want to group records by dates. For example, you can group records by month, quarter, or year.

When you open the Query Designer, it displays the query design grid and the Show Table dialog box. The Show Table dialog box lists all the tables and queries in the current database.

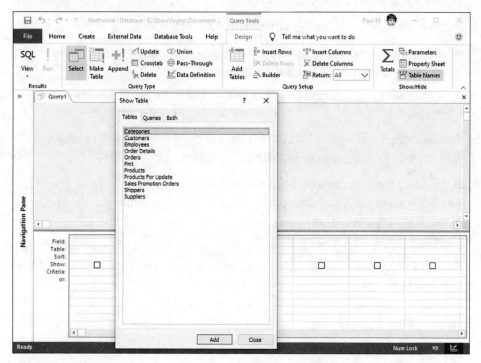

In Design view, you use Show Table to add one or more tables or queries to the query grid.

When you add more than a few tables to a query, you can reposition the field lists in the main pane of the Query Designer to view more clearly the relationship lines that link the tables. You add a field to the query by dragging it from the field list in the main pane to the Field row in a blank column in the grid at the bottom of the Query Designer, or you can select fields from the list displayed in the Field row. The asterisk at the top of the field list adds all the fields in a table to the query design grid.

By default, a query returns all matching records, but you can select a preset value (5, 25, 100, 5%, or 25%) or enter a value to specify how many records you want to display. By limiting the number of records, you can view data such as the top 20 orders that customers placed in the current month.

To create a select query by using the Simple Query Wizard

1. On the **Create** tab, in the **Queries** group, click **Query Wizard**.

2. In the **New Query** dialog box, with **Simple Query Wizard** selected in the list of wizards, click **OK**.

3. In the **Simple Query Wizard**, use the **Tables/Queries** list to select the first table or query you want to use for this query.

4. In the **Available Fields** list, do either of the following:

    -   Select the field or fields you want to include in the query, then click the arrow (>) to move the fields to the **Selected Fields** list.

    -   Click the chevron button (>>) to move all the fields to the **Selected Fields** list.

5. Repeat steps 3 and 4 to include other tables or queries in the select query and add the fields you want to include. Then click **Next**.

6. If the query includes numeric fields or fields from more than one table, the wizard prompts you to create a detail query or a summary query. A detail query is the default option. To continue creating a detail query, click **Next**. To create a summary query, do the following:

    Select the **Summary** option, then click **Summary Options** to display a list of the affected fields.

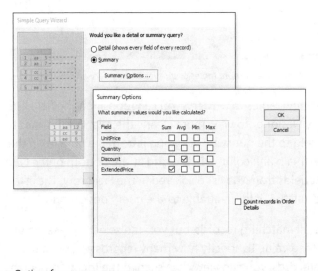

Options for a summary query.

In the **Summary Options** dialog box, select the check box for each summary function you want to apply to each of the fields.

Click **OK** to close the **Summary Options** dialog box and return to the wizard.

7. Click **Next** in the wizard.

8. If the query includes a Date/Time field, click an option to specify the way you want to group dates in the query, then click **Next**.

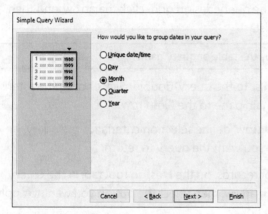

Options for grouping records by date.

9. On the wizard's last page, enter a name for the query, choose whether to open the query to review the results or open the query in Design view, and then click **Finish**.

To create a select query in Design view

1. On the **Create** tab, in the **Queries** group, click **Query Design**.

2. In the **Show Table** dialog box, select the tables or queries you want to use in the query. Click **Add** to add the objects to the **Query Designer**, then click **Close**.

3. To add fields to the query, do one of the following:

    *   From the field lists in the main pane, drag the fields you want to include in the query to the **Field** row in the query design grid. Access adds the field and table or query name to the grid.

        Tip You can display or hide the table row by clicking the Table Names button in the Show/Hide group on the Design tool tab.

        ---

    *   Click in the **Field** row of the query design grid, click the arrow, and then select the field from the list.

        Tip Each field is preceded by the table or query name.

        ---

    *   To add all fields in a field list to the query, double-click or drag the asterisk from the field list in the main pane to the **Field** row.

4. In the **Criteria** row and the **Or** row, define selection criteria for the query depending on which records you want the query to return.

5. To return a specific number of records, on the **Design** tool tab, in the **Query Setup** group, click the **Return** arrow, then select the option you want to apply or enter the value in the **Return** box.

6. On the **Quick Access Toolbar**, click **Save**.

7. In the **Save As** dialog box, enter a name for the query, then click **OK**.

Create crosstab queries

A crosstab query uses Sum, Avg, or another aggregate function to group a query's results. In Datasheet view, a crosstab query looks something like a PivotTable in Microsoft Excel. The query's data is grouped by two sets of values, based on fields you select. One set appears down the left side of the datasheet, and the other appears across the top. The values in the body of the query come from the field you designate as the Value field.

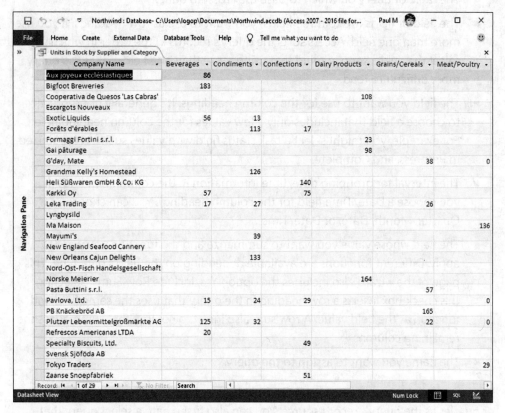

A crosstab query summarizing units in stock by supplier and category.

Access provides a wizard you can use to create a crosstab query, or you can use the Query Designer to specify the fields for the query and to define the calculations you want the query to perform. When you add fields to a crosstab query, you specify which fields to use as row headings (you can use as many as three fields), which field appears in the columns across the top, and which field is used for the summary values.

You can select fields from only one table or query when you use the Crosstab Query Wizard. To work around this limitation, you can create a select query that includes fields from multiple tables and then choose the select query as the record source when you work in the Crosstab Query Wizard.

In the wizard, you must identify the following information:

- The table or query on which to base the crosstab query.

- The field or fields (up to three fields) you want to use as row headings. If you use more than one field, Access sorts the query's records in the order in which you select the fields. Keep in mind that using more than one field makes the query more difficult to read.

- The field you want to use for the column headings. It's generally good practice to choose a field that includes only a few values for the column heading field. For example, you might select a task status field with values such as Not Started, In Progress, and Complete.

- The interval for grouping date/time information in the column headings (if you choose a Date/Time field for the column heading). You can choose Year, Quarter, Month, Date, or Date/Time.

- The field whose value you want to summarize and the function you want to apply. Different functions are available depending on the field's data type. This page of the wizard also includes the option Yes, Include Row Sums. Selecting this check box inserts a row heading in the query that uses the same field and function as the field value. A row sum also inserts a column that summarizes the remaining columns.

- The name you want to assign to the query.

When you create a crosstab query in Design view, you can include multiple tables or queries as the query's record source. You can also first create a select query that returns the records you want and use that query as the sole record source for the crosstab query.

See Also For information about creating select queries, see "Create select queries" earlier in this topic.

The design grid for a crosstab query contains a Total row and a Crosstab row (in addition to the Sort, Criteria, and Or rows you work with in select queries). You use the Crosstab row to specify which field or fields to use as row headings, which field to use for the query's column headings, and which field to summarize for the query's values. In the Total row, you specify the summary function that the query applies.

To create a crosstab query by using the Crosstab Query Wizard

1. On the **Create** tab, in the **Queries** group, click **Query Wizard**.

2. In the **New Query** dialog box, select **Crosstab Query Wizard**, then click **OK**.

3. On the wizard's first page, select the table or query on which to base the crosstab query, then click **Next**.

4. Specify the field or fields (up to three fields) you want to use as row headings, then click **Next**.

5. Select the field you want to use for the column headings, then click **Next**.

6. If you chose a **Date/Time** field for the column heading in step 5, specify the interval for grouping date/time information in the column headings, then click **Next**.

7. Select the field whose value you want to summarize and the function you want to apply, then click **Next**.

8. Enter a name for the query, then click **Finish**.

To create a crosstab query in Design view

1. On the **Create** tab, in the **Queries** group, click **Query Design**.

2. In the **Show Table** dialog box, select the tables or queries you want to use in the query. Click **Add** to add the tables to the **Query Designer**, then click **Close**.

3. From the table field lists, drag the fields you want to include in the query to the **Field** row in the query design grid. (You can also select fields from the list Access displays when you click in the **Field** row in the query design grid.)

4. In the **Criteria** row, define any selection criteria for the query.

5. On the **Design** tool tab, in the **Query Type** group, click **Crosstab**.

6. In the **Crosstab** row, specify the field or fields you want to use for row headings, column headings, and the query's values.

7. In the **Total** row for the value field, select the summary function you want to apply.

8. On the **Design** tool tab, in the **Results** group, click **Run** to display the query's results.

Create parameter queries

A parameter query provides flexibility in applying criteria. Instead of adding criteria such as = "*Los Angeles*" to the City field, you define a parameter for that field by using a format and a prompt such as *[Enter City Name]*. When you run a parameter query, Access opens the Enter Parameter Value dialog box, which displays the prompt you defined. You can enter the value you want to use as criteria (for example, *Minneapolis* or *Montreal* for the city parameter). Access returns the set of records that match the criteria you provide.

When you create a parameter query, you also specify the parameter's data type, which should match the data type for the field you defined the parameter for.

Tip You can also use parameters in crosstab, append, make-table, and update queries.

Use a parameter query to specify criteria when you run the query.

To create a parameter query

1. On the **Create** tab, in the **Queries** group, click **Query Design**.

2. In the **Show Table** dialog box, add the tables you want to use in the query.

3. Add the fields you need to the query.

4. In the **Criteria** row for the field you want to use as a parameter, enter the parameter prompt, enclosing the prompt in square brackets.

5. On the **Design** tool tab, in the **Show/Hide** group, click **Parameters**.

6. In the **Query Parameters** dialog box, in the **Parameter** column, enter the parameter prompt exactly as it appears in the design grid. In the **Data Type** column, select the data type for the parameter, then click **OK**.

Create action queries

Action queries are often used to help manage the records in a database. For example, you can use a select query to retrieve records for all discontinued products. You can use a make-table or an append query—two types of action queries—to archive those records. You can run an update or a delete query to update the value of a field or to remove records that match criteria you define.

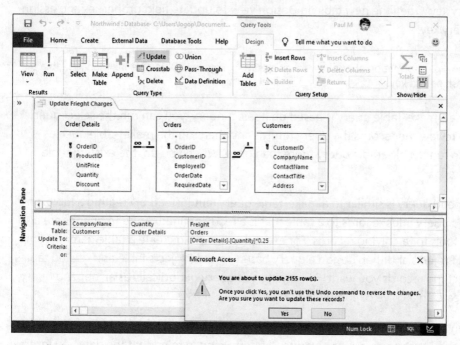

Access displays a warning before you run an action query.

When you run a make-table query, Access creates a table (in the current database or in another database you designate) that's defined by the fields included in the query. A make-table query has at least a couple of functions:

- A make-table query can improve the performance of your database when you find yourself frequently running a select query that is based on several tables whose data doesn't change. Access can run the select query more quickly if it is based on a single table (created by the make-table query) instead of on multiple tables.

- You can use a make-table query to build your data archives. For example, use a make-table query to store all the orders for the past year and use the Orders table only for current orders.

A table created by a make-table query inherits field names and data types but not all settings specified for other field properties. Also, the new table does not include a primary key. Open the new table in Design view to update field properties and assign a primary key.

See Also For information about how to set a primary key, see "Objective 1.2: Manage table relationships and keys."

Because a make-table query is based on a select query, you can run the select query first to review the records the query returns and then run the make-table query. You can run a make-table query more than once. When you do, the existing table is deleted.

An append query is similar to a make-table query, but instead of creating a table, an append query adds records to a table that is already defined. Append queries are also useful tools for archiving records. For example, you could create a table named Completed Projects and then design a query based on the Projects table and related tables to select the records you want. By running this query periodically as an append query, you create an archive of completed projects.

You can append records to a table in the current database or a different database you specify. When you create an append query, keep in mind that the data you insert by running the query must conform to the design of the destination table. After you designate a query as an append query, Access adds the Append To row to the query design grid. Based on the table you are appending records to, Access selects and displays a matching field in the Append To row. You can change the matching fields that

Access provides, but the data type and other properties of the field specified in the Append To row must be compatible with the field in the query. The source data must also conform to any validation rules defined for the destination table or the fields that the table contains.

As with make-table queries, you create an append query by first defining a select query. After setting up the select query, verify that it returns the records you need by running it. If the results are correct, you can then select the table you want to append records to.

Action queries can also be used to update or delete records. For example, you can use an update query to increase the values in a price field by a specified percentage or to perform date arithmetic by adding or subtracting a specific time period to the values in a date field. A delete query removes the set of records that meets criteria you define. You can use a delete query to remove all products marked Discontinued, for example.

To create an update query or a delete query, you start by creating a select query. For an update query, Access adds the Update To row to the design grid and removes the Sort and Show rows. In the Update To row for the field or fields you want to modify, you enter the expression that will update the field's current values. For example, to add 30 days to the ExpirationDate field, you would enter the expression **[ExpirationDate]+30**. When you run the update query, Access displays a message box telling you how many rows (records) will be updated.

IMPORTANT You cannot undo the changes made by an update query or a delete query. Before you run the query, you should make a backup copy of the table whose records will be updated or deleted. You can check which records will be affected before you run the query by switching the query to Datasheet view.

In a delete query, Access adds the Delete row to the query grid and removes the Show and Sort rows. In the Delete row, when you select the Where option for a field, you can specify criteria in the field's Criteria row that select the records Access will delete. For example, you might delete all records where the Discontinued field equals Yes or all task records for which the status is marked as complete.

When you work with delete queries, you might delete records you weren't expecting to. This occurs if the table you're deleting records from is related to another table and the tables' relationship is set up to use the Cascade Delete Related Records option. You can turn off this option if necessary by modifying the tables' relationship.

See Also For more information about the Cascade Delete Related Records option, see "Objective 1.2: Manage table relationships and keys."

To create and run a make-table query

1. Create a select query on which to base the make-table query.

   See Also For more information about how to create a select query, see "Create select queries" earlier in this topic.

2. With the select query open in Design view, on the **Design** tool tab, in the **Results** group, click **Run**.

3. Review the records returned by the select query in Datasheet view.

4. On the **Home** tab, in the **Views** group, click **View**, then click **Design View** to return the query to Design view.

5. On the **Design** tool tab, in the **Query Type** group, click **Make Table**.

6. In the **Make Table** dialog box, enter a name for the table, then do one of the following:

   - To have Access create the table in the current database, click **Current Database**.

   - To have Access create the table in another database, click **Another Database**. Then either enter the file name in the **File Name** box or click **Browse**, navigate to and select the file, and then click **OK** to return to the **Make Table** dialog box.

7. Click **OK** to close the **Make Table** dialog box.

8. On the **Design** tool tab, in the **Results** group, click **Run**.

9. In the **Microsoft Access** message box alerting you that you'll be pasting rows into a new table and the operation can't be undone, click **Yes**.

To create and run an append query

1. Create a select query on which to base the append query.

   See Also For more information about how to create a select query, see "Create select queries" earlier in this topic.

2. With the select query open in Design view, on the **Design** tool tab, in the **Results** group, click **Run**.

3. Review the records returned by the select query in Datasheet view.

4. On the **Home** tab, in the **Views** group, click **View**, then click **Design View** to return the query to Design view.

5. On the **Design** tool tab, in the **Query Type** group, click **Append** to open the **Append** dialog box.

6. If you want to add the records to a table in a different database, click **Another Database**, and then either enter the database name in the **File Name** box or click **Browse**, navigate to and select the file, and then click **OK**.

7. In the **Append** dialog box, expand the **Table Name** list and click the table you want to add the records to. Then click **OK**.

8. On the **Design** tool tab, in the **Results** group, click **Run**.

9. In the **Microsoft Access** dialog box asking you to confirm the operation, click **Yes**.

To create and run an update query

1. Create a select query on which to base the update query.

   See Also For more information about how to create a select query, see "Create select queries" earlier in this topic.

2. On the **Design** tool tab, in the **Query Type** group, click **Update**.

3. In the **Update To** row for the field or fields you want to update, enter an expression that calculates the updated values.

4. On the **Design** tool tab, in the **Results** group, click **Run**.

5. In the **Microsoft Access** dialog box asking you to confirm the operation, click **Yes**.

To create and run a delete query

1. Create a select query on which to base the delete query.

   See Also For more information about how to create a select query, see "Create select queries" earlier in this topic.

2. On the **Design** tool tab, in the **Query Type** group, click **Delete**.

3. In the **Delete** row, select **Where** for each field on which you want to apply criteria for the deletion.

4. In the **Criteria** row, specify the criteria for selecting the records you want to delete.

5. On the **Design** tool tab, in the **Results** group, click **Run**.

6. In the **Microsoft Access** dialog box asking you to confirm the operation, click **Yes**.

Create multiple-table queries

You can create a multiple-table query to return a set of records from related tables or from tables you join for the query itself. For example, you can join the Customers table to the Orders table by using the CustomerID field.

Whenever you have relationships defined between two tables, Access automatically joins the tables by using the fields in the defined relationships. Access also includes an option named Enable AutoJoin. This option is enabled by default, so when you create a query that includes tables that aren't directly related, Access tries to link the tables for you by examining the primary key fields for each table and then looking for a field with the same name and data type in one of the other tables in the query. If Access doesn't find a match, you can link the tables yourself. By joining the tables in this way, you link them for the purposes of designing and running the query. You don't create a permanent table relationship.

Tip You can toggle the Enable AutoJoin feature on and off from the Object Designers page of the Access Options dialog box.

See Also For more information about table relationships, see "Objective 1.2: Manage table relationships and keys."

To retrieve the records you need in a query, you use either an inner join or an outer join. The default join is an inner join. With an inner join, a query returns only records with matching rows in both tables. For example, a query that joins a projects table and a tasks table returns records only for projects that have assigned tasks and for tasks that are assigned to specific projects. By using an outer join in this query, you can retrieve the set of matching records (projects and their assigned tasks) in addition to projects without tasks (all projects) or tasks without projects (all tasks).

You can create a "left" outer join or a "right" outer join to retrieve all the records from one of the tables. *Left* and *right* refer to how the tables are identified in the Join Properties dialog box. Access provides options to create an outer join that returns all records from one table and matching records from another, depending on which table's records you want to view.

See Also For more information about joins, see "Set relationships" in "Objective 1.2: Manage table relationships and keys."

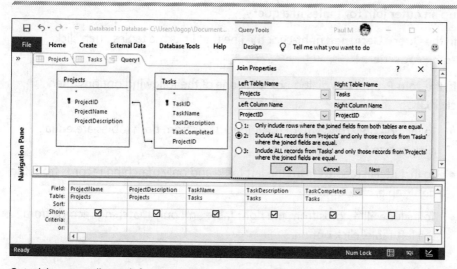

Outer joins return all records from one table and matching records from another.

Tip You can also specify the join type that related tables use when you have the Relationships window open. Click the relationship line for the tables you want to work with, then click Edit Relationships in the Tools group on the Relationship Tools Design tool tab. Click Join Type in the Edit Relationships dialog box, then click the option for the type of join you want to use.

To add tables to a query

➜ In the **Query Designer**, right-click an empty area of the main pane (not on a field list), then click **Show Table**.

Or

1. Open the query in Design view.

2. On the **Design** tool tab, in the **Query Setup** group, click **Show Table**.

3. In the **Show Table** dialog box, select the tables or queries you want to add, click **Add**, and then click **Close**.

To remove a table from a query

1. Open the query in Design view.

2. Right-click the field list for the table, then click **Remove Table**.

To set up an outer join for tables in a query

1. In the **Query Designer**, right-click the line that links the tables, then click **Join Properties**.

2. In the **Join Properties** dialog box, click one of the following options, then click **OK**:

   • To include only rows where the joined fields from both tables are equal, click option **1**.

   • To include all records from the left table and only matching records from the right table, click option **2**.

   • To include all records from the right table and only matching records from the left table, click option **3**.

Save queries

Access automatically saves a query you create by using one of the query wizards. The wizard provides a default name for the query based on the first (or only) table or query you select as the query's data source. When you design a query in the Query Designer, Access assigns a default name such as *Query1*. You can replace either default name with a more meaningful one. You cannot use the same name for a table and a query. To avoid this conflict, you can include a prefix such as *qry* in each query's name.

You can use options on the Save As page in the Backstage view to create a copy of a query as a new database object (a new query, form, or report) or as a PDF or an XPS file. Saving a query as a new database object can be helpful if you want to experiment with the query by adding additional selection criteria, for example, but don't want to risk inadvertent changes to the original query. A form or report you create by saving a query as a database object contains the query's fields and provides a starting point from which you can further develop the object you create. When you save a query as a PDF or an XPS file, you create a static copy of the query's data. You can specify a range of pages to save and also set accessibility options.

When you delete a query from a database, keep in mind that queries are often used as the record source for forms and reports. If you delete a query that is the basis of a form or report, you must update the record source before you can use the form or report to view records.

To save a query from Design view

1. On the **Quick Access Toolbar**, click **Save**.

2. In the **Save As** dialog box, enter a name for the query, then click **OK**.

To save a query as a database object

1. In the **Navigation Pane**, right-click the query, then click **Open**.

2. Click the **File** tab, then click **Save As**.

3. In the **File Types** list, click **Save Object As**.

4. In the **Save The Current Database Object** area, under **Database File Types**, click **Save Object As**, then click **Save As**.

5. In the **Save As** dialog box, in the **Save** QueryName **to** box, enter a name for the query.

Saving a query as a new database object.

6. In the **As** box, select **Query**, **Form**, or **Report**.

7. Click **OK**.

To save a query as a PDF or an XPS file

1. In the **Navigation Pane**, right-click the query, then click **Open**.

2. Click the **File** tab, then click **Save As**.

3. In the **File Types** list, click **Save Object As**.

4. In the **Save The Current Database Object** area, under **Database File Types**, click **PDF Or XPS**, then click **Save As**.

5. In the **Publish As PDF Or XPS** dialog box, in the **File Name** box, modify the name Access supplies if necessary.

6. In the **Save As Type** list, select **PDF** or **XPS Document**.

7. To set a page range or other options, click **Options**, specify the options you want to use, and then click **OK** in the **Options** dialog box.

8. In the **Publish As PDF Or XPS** dialog box, click **Publish**.

Objective 3.1 practice tasks

The practice file for these tasks is located in the **MOSAccessExpert2019\ Objective3** practice file folder. The folder also contains a result file that you can use to check your work.

➤ In the **AccessExpert_3-1** database, do the following:

❑ Use the Simple Query Wizard to create a query from the Categories table that includes only the CategoryName and Description fields. Name the query *Simplified Categories*. Choose the option to view information so that you can examine the query's results.

❑ Close the Simplified Categories query.

❑ Use the Query Designer to create a select query based on the Products table. Add the fields ProductName, CategoryID, and UnitPrice, and sort the CategoryID field in ascending order. Save the query as *Products by Category*.

❑ Use the Save As command to save Products by Category to a new query named *Update Product Prices*. Convert this query to an update query that increases unit prices by 10 percent. Save and close the query.

❑ Use the Query Designer to create a select query based on the Categories, Products, and Suppliers tables. Add the fields CategoryName from the Categories table, CompanyName from the Suppliers table, and UnitsInStock from the Products table. Save the query as *Units in Stock by Supplier and Category*. Run the query to display the records returned by the select query. Now convert this query to a crosstab query. Use the CompanyName field as the row heading field and the CategoryName field as the column heading field. Use the UnitsInStock field as the value field. Select Sum in the Total row for the UnitsInStock field. Save and close the query.

❑ Use the Query Designer to create a select query based on the Tasks and Projects tables. From the Tasks table, add the TaskName, TaskDescription, and TaskCompleted fields; from the Project table, add the ProjectName field. Run the query to display the results.

❑ Use the options in the Join Properties dialog box to create an outer join that shows all the records from the Projects table. Run the query again to view how the outer join changes the query's results.

➤ Open the **AccessExpert_3-1_results** database. Compare the two databases to check your work. Then close the open databases.

Objective 3.2: Modify queries

After you set up a query, you can modify it by renaming it, changing or rearranging the fields, showing and hiding query fields, and sorting the query's results. You can also format the fields in a query. This topic examines some of the ways you can modify a query.

Change the fields in a query

With a query open in Design view, you can add, remove, and rearrange the query's fields in several ways. To add fields, you can use the field list or the Field row in the design grid. When you drag a field between two fields already in the grid, Access moves the other fields in the query to the right. You can also use the options in the Show Table dialog box to add another table or query to the query and then include fields from those objects in the query's design. When you remove a field, you cannot use the Undo command to reverse this action.

You can also reposition the fields in a query design grid.

To add fields to a query

1. Open the query in Design view.

2. Do either of the following:

    - In the field list in the top pane of the **Query Designer**, select the field, then drag the field to the query design grid.

    - In the **Field** row in a blank column in the design grid, select the field you want to add.

To delete a field

→ In the design grid, click the field column header, then press **Delete**.

To insert a column in the design grid

1. In the query design grid, click in the column that you want to insert a new column to the left of.

2. On the **Design** tool tab, in the **Query Setup** group, click **Insert Column**.

To delete a column in the design grid

1. In the query design grid, click in the column that you want to delete.

2. On the **Design** tool tab, in the **Query Setup** group, click **Delete Column**.

To change the order of the fields in the design grid

→ Click the top of the column for the field you want to move (hold down the **Shift** key to select more than one column), then drag the column or columns to the new location.

Show and hide query fields

By default, the check box in the Show row for each field in a query is selected. This means that the values in each field are displayed in the query's results. By clearing this check box for a field, you remove that field's values from the query's result without removing the field from the query.

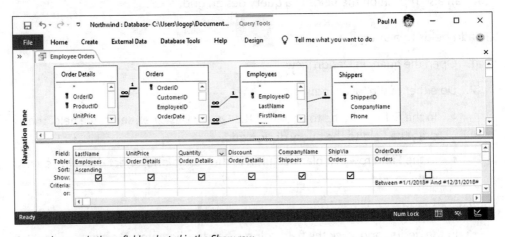

Access shows only those fields selected in the Show row.

The capability to hide a field is helpful when you want to use a field to define selection criteria or to sort a query but don't want to show the field in the query's results. Fields you use this way are essential to defining the query, but their values don't need to be shown in the query's results. You might add an ID field or a date field to a query for these purposes. For the ID field, you might specify a customer's ID. You could use the date field to sort records to filter orders to show only a time-based subset (such as your previous fiscal year). The purpose of these fields is to tailor the query—any reporting or analysis doesn't require that the query include the values that these fields provide.

To show and hide query fields

1. Open the query in Design view.

2. In the query design grid, clear the **Show** check box for any fields you want to hide.

3. Select the **Show** check box to display a field in the results.

Sort data within queries

You use the Sort row in the query design grid to specify how Access sorts the records returned by a query. You can sort by a single field or by more than one field. When you specify a sort order for more than one field, Access sorts records according to the order in which the fields appear left to right in the query design grid.

Tip If you add all the fields from a table or query to the query design grid by dragging the asterisk, you cannot use the Sort row to sort records.

If you want to sort by multiple fields in a specific sequence but also display one of these fields later in the order of the fields, you can add a second instance of the field, set the sort order for the field, and then hide the second instance of the field so that it doesn't appear in the query's results.

The sorting options are Ascending, Descending, and Not Sorted. Be sure to reposition fields as you want them to appear when you are sorting records by more than one field.

See Also For more information about how to rearrange field order, see "Change the fields in a query" earlier in this topic.

To use the Sort row in a query

1. Open the query in Design view.

2. In the query design grid, click in the **Sort** row for the field you want to sort by, click the arrow, and then select **Ascending**, **Descending**, or **Not Sorted**.

3. To sort by more than one field, specify the sort order for the additional fields. In the query design grid, arrange the fields from left to right in the order you want Access to use them to sort records.

3

Use operators

Access defines a set of operators you can use in expressions that define query criteria, filters, or calculated fields. The operators you can use include basic arithmetic operators for addition (+), subtraction (–), multiplication (/), and division (*). You can use the ampersand (&) to combine the values in two or more text fields. For example, the expression *[City] & ", " & [State/Province]* combines the City and State/Province fields in a single text string.

Access also provides logical operators, such as Or, And, and Not, and comparison operators, such as < (less than) and > (greater than). Here are a few examples of how to use these operators in criteria expressions.

Expression	Result
<Date()	Returns records with a date earlier than the current date
"Lee" or "Andersen"	Returns records with either Lee or Andersen as the value in the field
Not "Andersen"	Returns records except those with Andersen as the value in the field
Not <#4/1/2020#	Returns only records with a date later than 4/1/2020
<=50	Returns records with a value of 50 or less
<>"Beverages"	Returns records that do not equal Beverages in this field

Three other comparison operators are Like, In, and Between. The Like operator can be used to compare a field value to a text string. For example, the expression *Like "98###"* in a postal code field returns records with ZIP Code values that start with 98. You can use the In operator to find specific records. The expression *In ("Las Vegas")* returns records with the value *Las Vegas* in the city field. Use the Between operator to select records within a range of dates (*Between #1/1/2020# And #3/31/2020#*) or a range of numbers (*Between 1200 And 1500*).

Filter data within queries

A select query often includes criteria that defines the subset of records the query returns when you run it. For example, to find records for customers in a specific city, you can add the City field to the query and then enter an expression such as =*"CityName"* (where *"CityName"* is the city you want to examine) to the Criteria row. You must enclose text values in quotation marks.

To specify criteria for a date field, enclose the date (or dates) in pound signs (#). You can retrieve records for orders placed between two dates by using an expression such as *Between #4/1/2017# And #6/30/2017#*. You can also use comparison operators to retrieve records that are less than (<) or greater than (>) a certain numeric amount.

See Also For more information about the operators you can use in a query, see "Use operators" earlier in this topic.

When you enter criteria in the Criteria row for more than one field, the query selects only records that match the criteria in all those fields—for example, records that have a value in the Order Date field greater than 9/15/2020 and a value of Fabrikam for the Company Name field. You can set up OR criteria (to find records with a value of Fabrikam or Contoso in the Company Name field, for example) by entering the second criterion in the Or row (below the Criteria row).

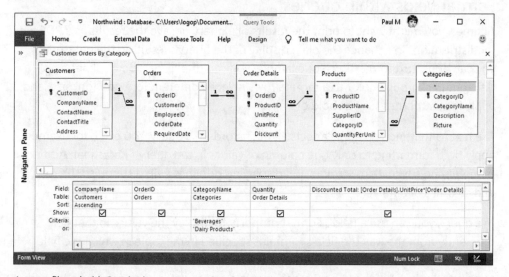

A query filtered with Or criteria.

You can filter the results of a query in Datasheet view by applying the filtering tools and options available for filtering records in a table.

See Also For more information about filtering results, see "Filter records" in "Objective 2.3: Manage table records."

To set filter criteria

1. In the query design grid, click in the **Criteria** row for the field you want to filter by.

2. Enter the expression for the criteria you want to apply to the field.

3. To define criteria for more than one field, do either of the following:

    *   To apply And criteria, click in the **Criteria** row for another field, then enter the expression to use as a filter.

    *   To apply Or criteria, click in the **Or** row for another field, then enter the expression to use as a filter.

4. Run the query to display the results.

Format fields within queries

At times, you might want to print the results of a query or save the results as a PDF file for distribution. To enhance the plain display of the query's results in the datasheet, you can apply text formatting. For example, you can display or hide gridlines, apply a different background color to alternate rows, select a different font and font size, and apply font attributes such as bold or italic.

The text formatting you apply affects all the records in a query. You can't, for example, apply bold formatting to only one column of values in the query's datasheet. Adding or modifying alternate row colors and displaying gridlines help distinguish the rows and columns of data.

In a query, you can use a field's Format property to display the values in that field differently from the way the field's format is specified in the table in which the field is defined. For example, a date field can be defined with the Short Date format in its table but displayed in the Long Date format in a query. You can also use a field's Caption property in a query to display a different label in the column heading. Setting the Format or Caption property for a field in a query does not define or change the property for the field in its table.

To apply text formatting to a query

1. Open the query in Datasheet view.

2. On the **Home** tab, in the **Text Formatting** group, do any of the following:

   • In the **Font**, **Font Size**, or **Font Color** list, select a different font, font size, or font color.

   • Click the **Bold**, **Italic**, or **Underline** button to format the text.

   • Click the **Background Color** arrow, then select a background color for odd-numbered rows.

   • Click the **Gridlines** arrow, then select to show both horizontal and vertical gridlines, only horizontal gridlines, only vertical gridlines, or no gridlines.

   • Click the **Alternate Row Color** arrow and select a color that is applied to even-numbered rows.

To set properties for a field in a query

1. Open the query in Design view.

2. On the **Design** tool tab, in the **Show/Hide** group, click **Property Sheet**.

3. Click in the column for the field you want to format.

4. In the property sheet, enter or select a value for properties such as **Format** and **Caption**.

3

Objective 3.2 practice tasks

The practice file for these tasks is located in the **MOSAccessExpert2019\ Objective3** practice file folder. The folder also contains a result file that you can use to check your work.

➤ Open the **AccessExpert_3-2** database.

➤ Open the Customer Orders By Category query in Design view, and make the following changes. Run the query after each change to check how the change affects the query's results.

  ❏ From the Products table, add the ProductName and UnitsInStock fields to the query.

  ❏ Hide the OrderID field.

  ❏ Sort the query in ascending order on the OrderDate field.

  ❏ Using operators, add criteria that filter the orders to those placed in 2019 in the Beverages and Dairy Products categories.

  ❏ Open the query in Datasheet view.

  ❏ Apply the *Blue, Accent 1* theme color as the alternating row color.

  ❏ Save and close the query.

➤ Open the **AccessExpert_3-2_results** database. Compare the two databases to check your work. Then close the open databases.

Objective group 4

Modify forms in Layout view

The skills tested in this section of the Microsoft Office Specialist Expert exam for Microsoft Access 365 and Microsoft Access 2019 relate to modifying and formatting forms. Specifically, the following objectives are associated with this set of skills:

4.1 Configure form controls

4.2 Format forms

The datasheet is a reasonable tool if you are entering only one or two records, but if you are entering a dozen records or even a hundred, you need to leave the datasheet behind and use the Access data-entry tool of choice: the form. A form is a collection of controls—usually labels and text boxes, but also lists, check boxes, and option buttons—each of which represents either a field or the name of a field. Forms make data entry easy and efficient.

Access provides tools that you can use to manage the size, position, alignment, and other properties of a form's controls. In addition, you can format a form so that it displays an image or displays the records in a specific sort order.

This chapter guides you in studying methods for using Layout view to configure form controls and format forms.

4

> To complete the practice tasks in this chapter, you need the practice files contained in the **MOSAccessExpert2019\Objective4** practice file folder. For more information, see "Download the practice files" in this book's Introduction.

Exam Strategy "Objective group 5: Modify reports in Layout view" covers Access reports. Forms and reports have important characteristics in common. When you modify and format reports, you apply many of the same skills that are covered in this chapter.

Objective 4.1: Configure form controls

This topic covers modifying form controls in Layout view. It describes how to add, remove, and move controls and how to work with properties that define a control's format and behavior. This section also covers how to manage form labels.

Add and remove controls

In Layout view, the Controls group on the Design tool tab displays an icon for each type of control you can use on a form. A ScreenTip identifies the type of control.

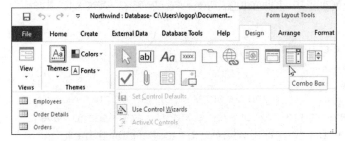

Form controls are identified by a ScreenTip.

See Also For a description of each type of control and related control properties, see the section "Set control properties" later in this task.

By default, Access enables the option Use Control Wizards and displays a wizard when you add a control such as a command button, combo box, or list box.

The Command Button Wizard prompts you to select a category (such as Record Navigation) and an action (such as Go To First Record or Find Record). In the Form Operations category, the actions include Close Form, Print A Form, and Refresh Form Data, among others. You can display a text label on the button or select from a group of images that depict the button's function—such as a small form icon for a button set up to open a form.

In the Combo Box Wizard and List Box Wizard, you specify the source of the list items (a table, a query, or a list that you define). You also need to specify whether Access should remember the value selected in the list (which you might use in an expression) or save the value in a specific field.

Other controls for which Access provides a wizard are the option group and the subform.

When you add a hyperlink control or a web browser control to a form, Access opens the Insert Hyperlink dialog box. This dialog box provides similar options for each of these types of controls. For a hyperlink control, you can link to a file or a webpage, another database object, or an email address. You can also build a link for either type of control by providing a base URL (such as *https://bing.com*), a path (such as *search*), and a parameter. For example, you might name a parameter **q** and give it the value **Microsoft+Office**, and the browser control would return search results related to Microsoft Office.

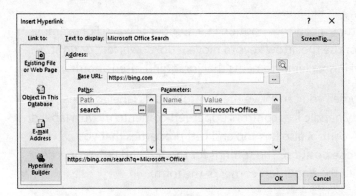

You can also use an expression to provide a value from a control on your form.

If a label is associated with a control, when you delete the control Access also deletes the label.

To add a control to a form

1. Open the form in Layout view.

2. On the **Design** tool tab, in the **Controls** group, click the icon for the type of control you want to add.

    Tip Point to controls to display their names in ScreenTips.

    ---

3. Click in the form where you want to place the control.

4. If Access displays a related control wizard, use the wizard to set up the control.

To remove a control from a form

→ Right-click the control, then click **Delete**.

→ Click the control to select it, then press **Delete**.

Move controls

You can change and fine-tune a control's position in a number of ways. For example, you can drag the control or use the arrow keys to move it up, down, left, or right. The arrow keys move a control in smaller increments than dragging often affords.

By dragging a control's border, you can move the control and its label together, or you can point to the larger gray handle in a control's upper-left corner to move a label or a control independently. A control also has Top and Left properties that you can set to move a control to a precise position. The settings for the Top and Left properties position a control relative to the upper-left corner of the form.

See Also For more information about control properties, see "Set control properties" later in this topic.

Moving a control.

In Layout view, a form's controls are contained within a layout that helps manage the alignment and arrangement of the controls. For desktop database forms, Access provides two default layouts. In the tabular layout, controls are arranged in columns and rows (something like a spreadsheet or a table). Labels are displayed in the form's Header section (similar to column headings). Access places the text box controls in the form's Detail section. In the stacked layout, controls appear in two columns, with labels in the column at the left and text box controls at the right. All the controls in the stacked layout are included in a single form section. Access uses the stacked layout for forms you create by using the Form command and for blank forms you create in Layout view.

By using the Move Up and Move Down commands in the Move group, you can reposition rows or a single cell in a layout. Another way to alter the arrangement of a layout is to merge or split cells. When you merge cells, one control spans two columns or rows. In contrast, when you split a cell in a layout, you can place two controls in that cell.

To move and position a control

→ Select the control, then do either of the following:

- Drag the control to its new position.
- Use the arrow keys to reposition the control.

To move a control in Layout view

1. Open the form in Layout view and click the control you want to reposition.
2. On the **Arrange** tool tab, in the **Move** group, click **Move Up** or **Move Down**.

To merge two cells in Layout view

1. Open the form in Layout view and select the cells you want to merge.
2. On the **Arrange** tool tab, in the **Merge/Split** group, click **Merge**.

To split a cell in Layout view

1. Open the form in Layout view and select the cell you want to split.
2. On the **Arrange** tool tab, in the **Merge/Split** group, click **Split Vertically** or **Split Horizontally**.

Set control properties

The properties for a form control are arranged on five tabs of the property sheet: Format, Data, Event, Other, and All. Form controls share some properties (such as the Name property), and each type of control also has specific properties related to its type. The following list describes some of the properties you often work with:

- **Format tab** Includes properties such as Caption, Height, Width, Text Align, and Visible. A control's Visible property shows or hides the control under conditions you define.

- **Data tab** Includes the Control Source property—the property that binds a control to data in a specific field or uses an expression to derive the control's data. Not all types of controls have a Control Source property. Bound controls (controls that are linked to a field) include text boxes, option groups (which contain option buttons or check boxes), combo boxes and list boxes, charts, and subforms and subreports. Unbound controls include labels, command and toggle buttons, tab controls, hyperlinks, the web browser control, lines, and images. The Data tab also includes properties such as Default Value, Validation Rule, and Validation Text.

  See Also For more information about field validation rules and the Default Value property, see "Objective 2.4: Create and modify fields."

- **Event tab** Lists properties such as On Click, Before Update, On Enter, and On Exit. You can associate a macro or a subprocedure written in Microsoft Visual Basic for Applications (VBA) with an event property to automate the operations of a form.

- **Other tab** Contains the Name property (in addition to other properties). You use the Name property to refer to a control in VBA code and in an expression. The Name property is not the same as the Caption property, which determines the display text associated with a control. Access creates a default value for the Name property (such as *Text10* or *List6*) when you add a control. You can update the Name property to make a control's purpose or relationship to a field clearer. You can use the ControlTip Text property on the Other tab to define the text for a ScreenTip that appears when you point to a control.

- **All tab** Displays all properties associated with a control.

Property sheet for a form control.

The following list describes the purpose of each form control available in Layout view and identifies additional control properties related to the type of control:

- **Text box** Displays text fields and general number and currency fields. In addition to using the Width and Height properties to specify the size of a text box control, you can format a text box by setting properties such as Back Color, Border Style, Border Width, Font Name, and Font Size. For a field that uses the Long Text data type, set the Scroll Bars property to Vertical to more easily review the text that's displayed.

- **Label** Identifies fields and controls on the form. Formatting properties for labels include Font Name, Font Size, Font Weight and Border Style, Border Width, and Border Color. You can use the Special Effect property to give the label a sunken or raised look.

- **Button** Used to perform an action such as opening another form, navigating to records, or running macros or VBA code. You can set a variety of formatting properties for buttons. For example, you can add a picture to a button. You can use the Hover Color and Pressed Color properties to specify the color of the button and its text when you point to or click the button.

- **Tab** Provides a set of pages on which you can organize related data. In a database that tracks projects, for example, you could use one page of a tab control for schedule information, a second for budget fields, and a third for displaying data about task assignments. You can set properties for the tab control in general and for each page (tab). You can add text boxes, list boxes, buttons, and other types of controls to a page to define and interact with the data it displays.

- **Hyperlink** Links to a file, a web page, or an email address. In a desktop database, you can also use a hyperlink to open another object in the database.

- **Web browser** Displays a file or a web page on a form.

- **Navigation** Provides buttons that you can link to forms or reports.

- **Combo box** Lets users select an item from a list or specify a new item. You can restrict users from entering new items by setting the control's Limit To List property to Yes. You can format a combo box by setting font and border properties. A combo box's data properties include the Row Source property, which specifies the list's values, and Row Source Type, which indicates whether the list comes from fields in a table or a query or is defined by a value list that you create. Access provides a wizard that helps you set up a combo box.

- **List box** Displays a list of values from a table or a query or from a list that you define. As with a combo box, you use the Row Source and Row Source Type properties to set up the list.

- **Check box** Specifies yes/no or true/false choices. A check box has fewer formatting properties than other types of controls. Use the Control Source property to bind the control to a field.

- **Attachment** Is bound to a field defined with the Attachment data type. Use the entries on the Format tab of the property sheet to specify border styles, height, width, and any special effects.

- **Subform/Subreport** Lets you embed another form or report within the form.

- **Image** Displays a logo or another type of image on a form.

By setting properties such as Back Color and Border Style in the property sheet, you can define or modify how a control appears. You can also set formatting properties for a control by working with commands on the Format tool tab when a form is open in Design view or Layout view. For example, in the Font group on the Format tool tab, you can make changes to font properties for labels and other controls on the form.

The alignment buttons in the Font group on the Format tool tab position the text in the label as flush left, flush right, or centered. In the Number group on the Format tool tab, you can apply a format to fields that use the Number, Currency, or Date/Time data type. For a date field, you can choose Medium Date, Long Date, Short Date, or another option from the Format list. The format you choose here affects how the date is displayed on the form, but it doesn't change the date format specified for the field in the table.

In the Control Formatting group on the Format tool tab, the Shape Fill command adds a background color to a control. You can use the Shape Outline command to modify the color and style of a control's borders. For a command button, you can use options on the Shape Effects menu to apply a shadow, a glow effect, or softened or beveled edges. Access enables the Change Shape command when you select a command button, tab control, or navigation button, for example. Use the options to display the button as an oval or another of the available shapes. For button controls, you can also apply a set of formats by choosing an option from the Quick Styles gallery.

To configure control properties

1. Open the form in Layout view.

2. On the **Design** tool tab, in the **Tools** group, click to enable the **Property Sheet** command. Access displays the form's property sheet.

3. At the top of the property sheet, in the **Selection type** list, click the control you want to configure.

4. On the **Format**, **Data**, **Event**, **Other**, or **All** tab of the property sheet, specify the values for the control properties you want to set.

To format form controls

1. Open the form in Layout view and select the control or controls you want to format.

2. On the **Format** tool tab, do one or more of the following:

- In the **Font** group, choose a new font, font size, or font color; apply bold, italic, or underline formatting; add a background fill color; or align the text.

- For **Number**, **Currency**, and **Date/Time** fields, use the options in the **Number** group to apply number, date/time, or currency formatting to the field.

3. In the **Control Formatting** group, do any of the following:

- Use the **Quick Style** and **Change Shape** commands to format a button.

- Use the **Shape Fill** command to add a background fill color to a control.

- Use the **Shape Outline** command to apply line styles and colors to the control's borders.

- Use the **Shape Effects** command to add a shadow or glow effect to a button control.

Manage labels

By default, Access includes a label when you add a control that can display data on a form. You can also use a label control for headings and to display descriptive or instructive text blocks on a form.

A label's Caption property is set by Access to match the Caption property set for a related field. You can change the text displayed in a label by selecting the label and editing the label's text. Access resizes the label to display the modified caption.

For a specific form, you can define the properties for a label control and then use those properties as default settings. (You can also set default control properties for other types of controls.) Some properties you might set are Fore Color, Background Color, Border Style, and Border Color.

To modify a label

1. Open the form in Layout view and open the form property sheet.

2. Add a label control to the form or select an existing label.

3. Edit the label text:

- Double-click the label to open it for editing and then make your changes.

- In the property sheet, use the **Caption** property to edit the label text.

4. Use options on the **Format** tool tab and on the **Format** tab of the property sheet to format the label as you want it to appear.

Objective 4.1 practice tasks

The practice file for these tasks is located in the **MOSAccessExpert2019\ Objective4** practice file folder. The folder also contains a result file that you can use to check your work.

➤ Open the **AccessExpert_4-1** database.

➤ Open the Products form in Layout view and do the following:

❑ Add a Combo Box control with the label Category that gets its values from the CategoryName field of the Categories table (sorted in ascending order) and stores selected values in the CategoryID field. In the property sheet of the new control, be sure to set the Allow Value List Edits property to No.

❑ Move the Category field and its label so that they appear between the Product Name and Supplier fields.

❑ Use the field list to add the UnitsInStock, UnitsOnOrder, and ReorderLevel fields to the form below the Supplier field.

❑ Add a command button control to the form.

❑ Configure the button to open the Order Details form and display all its records.

❑ Set the button caption to *Order Details* and name the button *OrderDetailsButton*.

❑ Add a hyperlink control below the Order Details button.

❑ Configure the hyperlink to send a message to your email address. In the Text To Display field, enter *Send reminder*. In the Subject field, enter *Check product reorders*.

❑ Save and close the Products form.

➤ Open the Orders form in Layout view and do the following:

❑ Change the font of all the text box controls to *Verdana*.

❑ Apply bold formatting to the Customer field.

❑ In the property sheet, apply the *Medium Date* format to the Order Date, Required Date, and Shipped Date fields.

❑ Change the Customer label to ***Customer Name***.

❑ Save and close the form.

➤ Open the **AccessExpert_4-1_results** database. Compare the databases to check your work. Then close the open databases.

Objective 4.2: Format forms

This topic describes some of the formatting features you can apply to a form. For example, it covers how to modify the tab order—the order in which you can move between controls by pressing the Tab key. It describes how to apply a theme to a form, how to insert images, and how to modify the background of a form. This topic also covers form properties related to sorting records in a form and printing a form.

Set tab order

Tab order determines the sequence in which controls gain focus as a user moves from field to field by pressing Tab. Carefully setting the tab order for a form can help users enter data in a logical manner (for example, first name, last name, and then middle initial instead of first name, street address, city, and then last name).

Access sets a default tab order as you add controls to a form, but this order might not be the most efficient. You can specify the tab order you want to use by setting the Tab Index and Tab Stop properties for a control in the control property sheet.

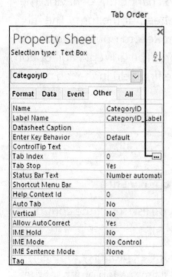

Use the Tab Index and Tab Stop properties to set a control's tab order.

On the Other tab of the property sheet for a control, two properties control tabbing for the control:

- **Tab Index** Specifies the order in which Access navigates the controls when you press Tab. The first control uses an index of 0 (zero), the second control has an index of 1, and so on. Note, as well, that when the property has the focus, Access displays the Tab Order button (...). Clicking this button opens the Tab Order dialog box, which lists each section of the form and the fields and controls within that section. The fields are listed in the current tab order. The dialog box describes how to reorder the rows to set the tab order for the form. The Auto Order button creates a tab order that reflects the position of controls as they appear left to right and top to bottom on a form.

- **Tab Stop** When this property is set to Yes, Access includes the control in the Tab navigation; when this property is set to No, Access skips the control during Tab navigation.

When you press Tab in the last control in the tab order, Access by default displays the next record in the form record source and then moves the focus to the first field in the tab order. You can use the Cycle property for a form to change this behavior. The Cycle property appears on the Other tab in the property sheet for the form. The All Records setting provides the default behavior. The Current Record option returns the focus to the first field in the tab order for the current record. The Current Page option (which applies to multipage forms) moves the focus to the first field in the tab order on the current page.

To set tab order properties for a control

1. Open the form in Layout view.

2. On the **Design** tool tab, in the **Tools** group, click **Property Sheet**.

3. At the top of the property sheet, in the **Selection Type** list, select the control whose properties you want to set.

4. On the **Other** tab of the property sheet, set the **Tab Index** property to specify the tab position of this control. To exclude a control from the tab order, set the **Tab Stop** property to **No**.

To set the Cycle property for a form

1. Open the form in Layout view.

2. On the **Design** tool tab, in the **Tools** group, click **Property Sheet**.

3. At the top of the property sheet, in the **Selection type** list, select **Form**.

4. On the **Other** tab of the property sheet, set the **Cycle** property to **All Records**, **Current Record**, or **Current Page**.

Sort records

When you base a form on a table or a query, the form inherits any sort order defined for its record source. You can change the sort order for the records in a form without changing the sort order specified in its record source. To do this, you use the Order By and Order By On Load properties.

These properties appear on the Data tab in a form property sheet. In the Order By property, you can enter the name of the field (enclosed in brackets) by which you want to sort the records. You can use more than one field by separating field names with a comma. By default, records are sorted in ascending order. Enter **DESC** after a field's names to sort in descending order.

The setting you specify for the Order By property is saved with the form, but the sort order is not automatically applied when you open the form unless you set Order By On Load to Yes.

Tip When you have a form open in Datasheet view, you can sort records by selecting a field and then clicking the appropriate Sort button in the Sort & Filter group on the Home tab.

To set the Order By and Order By On Load properties

1. Open the form in Layout view and open the form property sheet.

2. On the property sheet, in the **Selection Type** list, click **Form**.

3. On the **Data** tab of the property sheet, click in the **Order By** box, then enter the name of the field or fields you want to sort by, enclosing the field names in brackets and separating field names by using commas.

4. To sort a field in descending order, enter **DESC** after the field's name.

5. To sort the records when the form is opened, set **Order By On Load** to **Yes**.

4

Control form positioning

When a form is open in Layout view, you can use options in the Position group on the Arrange tool tab to adjust the margins around the text displayed by a control, the spacing between controls, and how controls are anchored within the layout.

Your forms will be more attractive and easier to use if the controls have some extra space within them. You can ensure this by adjusting the *margin*, which is the amount of space inside a field's box between the border and the text. You can adjust the margins for individual fields, but forms look better if all the fields have the same margins. Each setting on the Control Margins menu—None, Narrow, Medium, and Wide— progressively increases the space between the upper-left corner of a control and the position of the control text. The Wide setting can obscure text in a text box that is less than approximately 0.3 inches in height (assuming the font size you are using is the default 11 points).

In a stacked or tabular layout, *padding* refers to the amount of space outside the box. When you adjust the padding, you change the amount of space between fields and between a field and its label. Settings in the Control Padding area (also None, Narrow, Medium, and Wide) affect the space between controls in the layout.

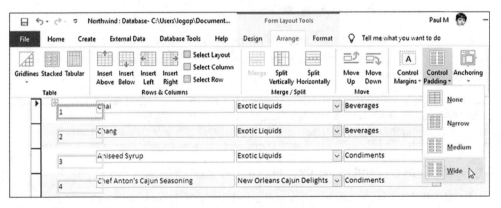

Adjust padding to space controls on a form.

Resizing a form window can affect how controls are arranged. By applying one of the anchoring options that Access provides, you can fasten controls to the top left (the default position), top right, bottom left, or one of the other anchoring positions. After you select an anchoring option, resize the form window to test the effect. You can anchor the entire layout or specific elements on a form. For example, if you add a line to set off a section of a form, apply the Stretch Across Top anchoring option to have the line stretch across the top of the form when the form window is resized.

To specify margins for text boxes on a form in Layout view

1. Open the form in Layout view and select the control you want to adjust.

2. On the **Arrange** tool tab, in the **Position** group, click **Control Margins**, then click a margin value: **None**, **Narrow**, **Medium**, or **Wide**.

Tip For more precise adjustments of a control's margins, on the Design tool tab, in the Tools group, click to enable the Property Sheet command. In the Property Sheet pane, click the Format tab, then use the Top Margin, Bottom Margin, Left Margin, and Right Margin properties to set the margins for the control.

To insert padding between controls on a form in Layout view

1. Open the form in Layout view and select the control you want to adjust.

2. On the **Arrange** tool tab, in the **Position** group, click **Control Padding**, then click a padding value: **None**, **Narrow**, **Medium**, or **Wide**.

Tip For more precise adjustments of a control's padding, on the Design tool tab, in the Tools group, click to enable the Property Sheet command. In the Property Sheet pane, click the Format tab, then use the Top Padding, Bottom Padding, Left Padding, and Right Padding properties to set the margins for the control.

To apply an anchoring option to a form

1. Open the form in Layout view and select the control you want to adjust.

2. On the **Arrange** tool tab, in the **Position** group, click **Anchoring**, then choose the option you want to apply.

Insert form headers and footers

A form includes three sections: Detail, Header, and Footer. When you first create a form in Layout view, Access displays the Header and Detail sections. You can use options in the Header/Footer group on the Design tool tab to insert a logo, a title, and the date and time (in various formats) in your form. The options add the form element to the form's Header section, but you can drag the form element to the footer section to include it there.

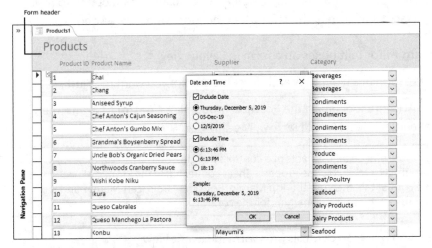

Adding the date and time to a form header.

Tip You can display or hide the Header and Footer sections in Design view by right-clicking in the Detail section of the form and then clicking Form Header/Footer.

The commands in the Header/Footer group insert built-in elements, but you can add other controls to a form's header or footer. For example, you can add button controls to the header or footer section to save room for text boxes and other controls in the Detail section.

See Also For more information about adding form controls, see "Add and remove controls" in "Objective 4.1: Configure form controls."

To insert information in a form header or footer

1. Open the form in Layout view.

2. On the **Design** tool tab, in the **Header/Footer** group, do any of the following:

   - To add a logo to the form header, click **Logo**. In the **Insert Picture** dialog box, navigate to and select the logo image file, then click **Open**.

   - To add a title to the form header, click **Title**. In the **Auto_Header()** control that appears, replace the default title with the title you want.

- To add the date or time to the form header, click **Date and Time**. In the **Date and Time** dialog box, select the check boxes for the elements you want to include, select the element formats you want, and then click **OK**.

Insert images

Forms can display logos or images related to the purpose of the database—product thumbnails, project locations, or employee portraits, for example. You can also insert an image as the background for a form.

You should update settings for the following properties that affect the appearance and behavior of the image (note that the settings in one or more of these properties affect the options for others):

- **Picture Type** Use the Embedded option if you want Access to add a copy of the image to the form. With this option, you know the image is available whenever you load the form, but adding a copy of the image increases the size of the form and the database. If you choose Link, Access uses the path and file name specified in the Picture property to locate the image file each time you open the form. If the file is moved, Access displays it only after you update the path. If you use the Shared option, Access adds a copy of the image to a system table. You can then select the image from the Picture property list to display it as a background in other database objects.

- **Picture** This property specifies the image file used as the background. You can choose an image from the list or click the ellipsis if you want to select a different image file.

- **Picture Tiling** If you set the Picture Size Mode property to Clip or Zoom and the image you insert is smaller than the form's dimensions, set this property to Yes to display multiple copies of the image on the form.

- **Picture Alignment** When the Picture Size Mode property is set to Clip or Zoom, you can choose an option in the Picture Alignment property to center the image or place it in a corner of the form.

- **Picture Size Mode** This property controls the size at which Access displays the image. The options include the following:

  - **Clip** Access trims the borders of the image so that it fits the size of the form.

  - **Zoom** Access increases or decreases the size of the image to fit the size of the form. With this option, Access retains the proportions of the image.

4

- **Stretch, Stretch Horizontal, Stretch Vertical** When you choose one of these options, Access resizes the image to fit the size of the form, but the image's proportions can be distorted.

To insert an image on a form

1. Open the form in Layout view.

2. On the **Design** tool tab, in the **Controls** group, click **Insert Image**, then do either of the following:

   - Select an image in the **Image** gallery.

   - Click **Browse** to locate the image file you want to use. Select the image file in the **Insert Picture** dialog box, then click **OK**.

3. Click the form at the position where you want the image to appear.

4. Open the form property sheet. At the top of the property sheet, in the **Selection Type** list, click the image name.

5. On the **Format** tab of the property sheet, set the values you want to use for the following properties: **Picture Type, Picture, Picture Tiling, Picture Alignment**, and **Picture Size Mode**.

To add an image to a form's background

1. Open the form in Layout view.

2. On the **Format** tool tab, in the **Background** group, click **Background Image**, then do either of the following:

   - Select an image in the **Image** gallery.

   - Click **Browse** to locate the image file you want to use. Select the image file in the **Insert Picture** dialog box, then click **OK**.

3. Open the form property sheet. At the top of the property sheet, in the **Selection Type** list, click **Form**.

4. On the **Format** tab of the property sheet, set the values you want to use for the following properties: **Picture Type, Picture, Picture Tiling, Picture Alignment**, and **Picture Size Mode**.

Objective 4.2 practice tasks

The practice files for these tasks are located in the **MOSAccessExpert2019\ Objective4** practice file folder. The folder also contains a result file that you can use to check your work.

➤ Open the **AccessExpert_4-2** database and do the following:

❑ Open the Products form in Layout view.

❑ Open the property sheet and exclude the ProductID and ReorderLevel controls from the tab order.

❑ Modify the form's tab order so that it follows this sequence: ProductName, Category, SupplierID, UnitsInStock, UnitsOnOrder, and OrderDetailsButton.

❑ Sort the records in descending order by product name.

❑ Set the form's control padding to Medium.

❑ Set the control margins to Narrow for all the input controls.

❑ Add the date and time to the Header section of the form. In the report's property sheet, select the formats *Short Date* and *Short Time,* respectively.

❑ Add the **AccessExpert_4-2** image (.jpg) to the Products form as a background image that uses the Stretch picture size mode.

❑ Save and close the form.

➤ Open the **AccessExpert_4-2_results** database. Compare the databases to check your work. (Note, however, that the results database does not show the background image in the Products form.) When you are done, close the databases.

Objective group 5

Modify reports in Layout view

The skills tested in this section of the Microsoft Office Specialist Expert exam for Microsoft Access 365 and Microsoft Access 2019 relate to modifying and formatting reports. Specifically, the following objectives are associated with this set of skills:

5.1   Configure report controls

5.2   Format reports

You can use reports to create a filtered view of your data, to group and summarize data, and to provide data in a format that's suitable for sharing, printing, and presentations. You configure reports and report elements by grouping and sorting records, adding controls, and adding and modifying labels. You format a report by displaying its data in multiple columns, positioning and formatting report elements, selecting a report orientation, adding information to the report header and footer, and inserting images on the report.

This chapter guides you in studying ways of configuring report controls and formatting reports.

5

To complete the practice tasks in this chapter, you need the practice files contained in the **MOSAccessExpert2019\Objective5** practice file folder. For more information, see "Download the practice files" in this book's introduction.

‹‹

Exam Strategy Forms and reports have many characteristics in common, and many of the tools you use to modify the design and formatting of reports are the same as those you use to modify forms. Be sure to study "Objective group 4: Modify forms in Layout view," for detailed information about topics such as working in Layout view, using the controls that Access offers, and modifying image layout properties. This chapter provides references to sections in Objective group 4 that describe these and other topics.

‹‹

Objective 5.1: Configure report controls

This topic describes how to work with fields and controls in a report. It explains how to group and sort records, add controls, and work with labels.

Group and sort records

Specifying how records are grouped in a report is an important aspect of the report's design. You can set grouping levels when you use the Report Wizard and by using the Group & Sort command when you work with a report in Layout view.

When you group records in Layout view, you work in the Group, Sort, And Total pane at the bottom of the report window. You can add one or more group header sections to the report based on the fields the report contains. The advantage of working in Layout view rather than Design view is that Access displays more clearly how the selections you make in the Group, Sort, And Total pane affect the report's organization. Access doesn't show this level of detail in Design view.

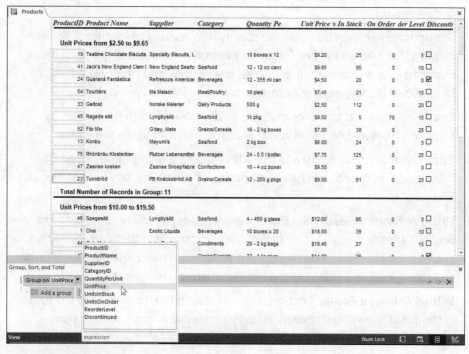

Grouped records.

You can sort records within each grouping level. For example, in a budget report, you could group records first by country or region and then sort records within that group by expense category. You could also group by expense category and sort records within that group by the date of the expense.

The More arrow in the Group, Sort, And Total pane displays additional options that you can set for grouping and sorting fields.

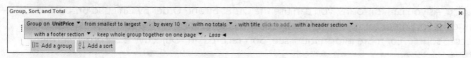

Additional options for grouping, sorting, and summarizing records.

The following list describes the options as Access displays them, left to right:

- **Sort Order** Use this option to specify the sort order, either ascending or descending.

- **Group Interval** Use this option to specify how records are grouped. You can group a text field on the first letter, for example, which would group all items that start with A together, all items that start with B, and so on. Date fields can be grouped by day, week, month, quarter, or an interval you define.

- **Totals** You can add totals for multiple fields and apply different summary functions (Sum and Avg or Min and Max, for example) to the same field.

- **Title** Use this option to change the title of the field being summarized. The title is used for the column heading and for labeling summary fields in headers and footers.

- **With/Without a Header Section** Use this setting to add or remove the header section for each group. Access moves the grouping field to the header when you add the header section. Access prompts you to remove any controls (other than the grouping field) from the header when you remove it.

- **With/Without a Footer Section** Use this setting to add or remove the footer section that follows each group. When you remove a footer section that contains controls, Access asks for confirmation to delete the controls.

- **Keep Group Together** The settings for this option determine how groups are laid out on the page when the report is printed.

The options available for summarizing field values depend on the data type of the field you select. For numeric fields, the range of options include Sum, Avg, Count, Max, and Min. For text and Date/Time fields, the Count options are available—either Count Values or Count Records. For a summary report, you can use the Hide Details option in the Grouping & Totals group to show only the summary fields.

See Also As you can for forms, you can use the Order By and Order By On Load properties to change the sort order for the records in a report without changing the sort order specified in its record source. For more information, see "Sort records" in "Objective 4.2: Format forms."

To group and sort records in a report

1. Open the report in Layout view.

2. On the **Design** tool tab, in the **Grouping & Totals** group, click **Group & Sort**.

3. In the **Group, Sort, And Total** pane, do the following:

   Click **Add A Group**, then select the field to group by.

   Click **More**, then specify settings for sorting, grouping intervals, totals, title, header and footer sections, and how to keep groups together on the page.

To summarize values on a report

1. Open the report in Layout view.

2. In the report, select the field you want to summarize.

3. On the **Design** tool tab, in the **Grouping & Totals** group, click **Totals**, then choose the summary function you want to apply.

Add controls to a report

Reports are designed primarily to present and share data (unlike forms or tables, which you use to enter, update, and delete data). For a report, you often work only with label and text box controls to identify and present data. For example, you might add a label to identify a summary field in a group header section or to provide a title in the Report Header section. You can add a text box to a report and then write an expression to create a calculated field. You can add an image control to enhance the appearance of a report. When you are adding controls in Layout view, you can expand the area of a layout by inserting rows or columns.

See Also For more information about how to work with specific controls, including how to use the control wizards, see "Objective 4.1: Configure form controls."

Although the data is more static in a report than in a form or a table, you can use a command button to perform an action related to the report or add a hyperlink control to display a website or an email address. In Report view, command buttons and hyperlinks are operational. In print preview, Access doesn't display a command button, and a hyperlink appears as static text.

In Design view, you can insert a subreport into a main report to provide related information. You can create the subreport by using the Report Wizard or by using the Subreport Wizard. In either case, the subreport must contain a field you can use to link it to the main report.

5

The Subreport Wizard appears when you add a subreport control to the report page. In the wizard, you can select a report you want to use as the subreport or select an option to base the subreport on an existing table or query.

To add controls to a report

1. Open the report in Layout view.

2. On the **Design** tool tab, click **Controls**. In the **Controls** gallery, click the type of control you want to add, then click in the report page where you want to add the control.

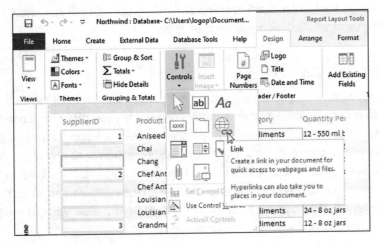

The report Controls gallery.

3. If prompted, work with the control wizard for the type of control you are adding.

To insert a subreport control

1. Open the main report in Design view.

2. On the **Design** tool tab, click **Controls**. In the **Controls** gallery, select the **Subform/Subreport** control, then click in the main report where you want to place the subreport.

3. Follow the steps in the **Subreport Wizard** to select the report, table, or query on which to base the subreport, select fields for the subreport, and specify the field that links the subreport and the main report.

To work with control layouts in Layout view

→ On the **Arrange** tool tab, in the **Table** group, do any of the following:

- To apply a different layout to the report, select all the fields in the report, then click **Stacked** or **Tabular**.

- To insert a row in the layout, click a cell in the adjacent row. In the **Rows & Columns** group, click **Select Row**, then click **Insert Above** or **Insert Below**.

- To insert a column in the layout, click a cell in the adjacent column. In the **Rows & Columns** group, click **Select Column**, then click **Insert Left** or **Insert Right**.

Add and modify labels

When you add a text, number, or date field to a report, Access creates a text box to display the field's data and creates an associated label to display the field's name or caption. (Access also creates an associated label for other types of fields, including lookup fields and fields that use the AutoNumber data type.) You can then use the techniques described elsewhere in this chapter to format, size, and position the labels to fit the report's design.

See Also For more information, see "Add controls to a report" earlier in this topic and "Format report elements" in "Objective 5.2: Format reports."

To work with the full range of properties available for a label control, open the property sheet. Specify values on the Format tab of the property sheet for properties such as Width, Height, Back Style, Special Effect, and Font Size. On the Other tab of the property sheet, you can replace the default label name.

You can also add labels to a report (or a form) that aren't associated with fields. You might use a freestanding label to provide instructional text or to display a heading in a report.

When you add a label to the Detail section of a report, Access might display a trace error button. In the Detail section, labels in most cases are associated with controls that display data, so Access considers the addition of an independent label an error because it detects that the label is not associated with another control. You can ignore the error Access detects or select an option to create an association and then specify the field.

5

You can turn off the error-checking options related to labels on the Object Designers page of the Access Options dialog box.

See Also For information about setting a default format for labels, see "Manage labels" in "Objective 4.1: Configure form controls."

To add a label

1. Open the report in Layout view.

2. On the **Design** tool tab, in the **Controls** group, click **Controls**, then click the **Label** control.

3. Click in the report where you want the label to appear.

4. Enter the text for the label.

To turn off error checking for labels

1. Open the **Access Options** dialog box and display the **Object Designers** page.

2. In the **Error checking in form and report design view** section, clear the **Check For Unassociated Label And Control** And **Check For New Unassociated Labels** check boxes.

3. Click **OK**.

Objective 5.1 practice tasks

The practice file for these tasks is located in the **MOSAccessExpert2019\
Objective5** practice file folder. The folder also contains a result file that you
can use to check your work.

➤ Open the **AccessExpert_5-1** database. If the Info Bar opens below
the ribbon, click the *Enable Content* button.

➤ Open the Products report in Layout view and do the following:

❏ Group the report data by unit price, smallest to largest, in
intervals of 10.

❏ Add a total for the units in stock. Select the options to show the
grand total and to show the subtotals in the group footers.

❏ Add a group for the category.

❏ Sort the report by unit price, smallest to largest.

❏ Save and close the report.

➤ Open the Sales for 2019 report in Design view and do the following:

❏ Using the Controls group and the Subform/Subreport Wizard, add
the Sales for 2019 Subreport as a subreport control. Insert the control
in the blank space at the top of the ShippedDate Header. Note that
this subreport does not need to be linked to a field in the main form.

❏ Change the *Sales by Year* label to **Sales for 2019**.

❏ Open the report in Report view to see your work, and then save and
close the report.

➤ Open the **AccessExpert_5-1_results** database. Compare the two
databases to check your work. Then close the open databases.

Objective 5.2: Format reports

You can use a variety of tools and techniques to format a report and the controls that you include on a report. For example, you can arrange a report's data in two or more columns, modify the control positioning, or add an image. You can also change the page orientation of the report, and you can add information to the report header and footer. This topic describes these and other aspects of formatting a report.

Format a report into multiple columns

When you want to set up a report in more than one column, you need to consider the number of fields the report contains, the width of report controls, and the page size. Columnar reports are best used for lists, directories, or other types of reports that include only a few fields. Stacking the fields (by using the stacked layout, for example) can also save space.

Products in Columns		

Products Report

Product Name	Chai	Product Name	Chang	Product Name	Aniseed Syrup
Supplier	Exotic Liquids	Supplier	Exotic Liquids	Supplier	Exotic Liquids
Category	Beverages	Category	Beverages	Category	Condiments
Quantity Per Unit	10 boxes x 20 bags	Quantity Per Unit	24 - 12 oz bottles	Quantity Per Unit	12 - 550 ml bottles
Unit Price	$18.00	Unit Price	$19.00	Unit Price	$10.00
Units In Stock	39	Units In Stock	17	Units In Stock	13
Units On Order	0	Units On Order	40	Units On Order	70

Product Name	Chef Anton's Cajun Seasoning	Product Name	Chef Anton's Gumbo Mix	Product Name	Grandma's Boysenberry Spread
Supplier	New Orleans Cajun Delights	Supplier	New Orleans Cajun Delights	Supplier	Grandma Kelly's Homestead
Category	Condiments	Category	Condiments	Category	Condiments
Quantity Per Unit	48 - 6 oz jars	Quantity Per Unit	36 boxes	Quantity Per Unit	12 - 8 oz jars
Unit Price	$22.00	Unit Price	$21.35	Unit Price	$25.00
Units In Stock	53	Units In Stock	0	Units In Stock	120
Units On Order	0	Units On Order	0	Units On Order	0

Product Name	Uncle Bob's Organic Dried Pears	Product Name	Northwoods Cranberry Sauce	Product Name	Mishi Kobe Niku
Supplier	Grandma Kelly's Homestead	Supplier	Grandma Kelly's Homestead	Supplier	Tokyo Traders
Category	Produce	Category	Condiments	Category	Meat/Poultry
Quantity Per Unit	12 - 1 lb pkgs.	Quantity Per Unit	12 - 12 oz jars	Quantity Per Unit	18 - 500 g pkgs.
Unit Price	$30.00	Unit Price	$40.00	Unit Price	$97.00
Units In Stock	15	Units In Stock	6	Units In Stock	29
Units On Order	0	Units On Order	0	Units On Order	0

Tuesday, December 10, 2019   Page 1 of 9

A three-column report.

On the Columns tab of the Page Setup dialog box, you use the Grid Settings area to specify the number of columns and the space between rows and columns. The Width and Height boxes in the Column Size area adjust column dimensions. The Same As Detail option fits the columns within the Detail section of the report. You also specify a setting for the column layout so that the data in the columns runs down the page and then across, or across the page and then down.

To specify column settings for a report

1. Open the report in Layout view.

2. On the **Page Setup** tool tab, in the **Page Layout** group, click **Columns**.

3. On the **Columns** tab of the **Page Setup** dialog box, specify the number of columns, the row and column spacing, the column size, and the column layout option, and then click **OK**.

Setting up a columnar report.

4. Display the report in Print Preview mode to test the settings.

Modify report positioning

When a report is open in Layout view, you can use options in the Position group on the Arrange tool tab to adjust the margins around the text displayed by a control and the spacing between controls.

Your reports will be more attractive if the controls have some extra space within them. You can ensure this by adjusting the *margin*, which is the amount of space inside a field's box between the border and the text. You can adjust the margins for individual fields, but reports look better if all the fields have the same margins. Each setting on the Control Margins menu —None, Narrow, Medium, and Wide—progressively increases the space between the upper-left corner of a control and the position of the control text. The Wide setting can obscure text in a text box that is less than approximately 0.3 inches in height (assuming the font size you are using is the default 11 points).

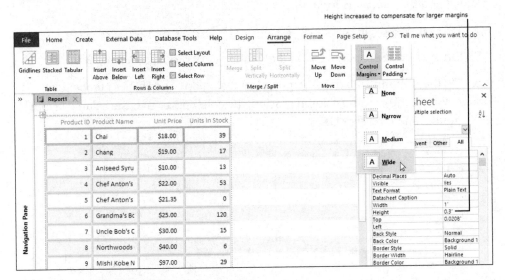

Use margins to adjust space inside controls on a report.

In a stacked or tabular layout, *padding* refers to the amount of space outside the box. When you adjust the padding, you change the amount of space between fields and between a field and its label. Settings in the Control Padding area (also None, Narrow, Medium, and Wide) affect the space between controls in the layout.

To specify margins for text boxes on a report in Layout view

1. Open the report in Layout view and select the control you want to adjust.

2. On the **Arrange** tool tab, in the **Position** group, click **Control Margins**, then click a margin value: **None**, **Narrow**, **Medium**, or **Wide**.

Tip For more precise adjustments of a control's margins, on the Design tool tab, in the Tools group, click to enable the Property Sheet command. In the Property Sheet pane, click the Format tab, then use the Top Margin, Bottom Margin, Left Margin, and Right Margin properties to set the margins for the control.

To insert padding between controls on a report in Layout view

1. Open the report in Layout view and select the control you want to adjust.

2. On the **Arrange** tool tab, in the **Position** group, click **Control Padding**, then click a padding value: **None**, **Narrow**, **Medium**, or **Wide**.

Tip For more precise adjustments of a control's padding, on the Design tool tab, in the Tools group, click to enable the Property Sheet command. In the Property Sheet pane, click the Format tab, then use the Top Padding, Bottom Padding, Left Padding, and Right Padding properties to set the margins for the control.

Format report elements

You can make changes to font properties for labels and other controls on a report. You can also change the size of the font, choose a different font color, or apply a background color to a control. Use the alignment buttons to position the text flush left, flush right, or centered.

Tip To select a report control for formatting, select the control from the Object list in the Selection group on the Format tool tab.

On the Format tool tab, in the Number group, you can apply a format to fields that use the Number, Currency, or Date/Time data type. The format you choose here affects how the date is displayed, but it does not change the date format specified for the field in the table.

With the commands in the Control Formatting group on the Format tool tab, you can format controls in other ways. The Shape Fill command adds a background color to a control, such as the report's title. The Shape Outline command provides options for modifying the color and style of a control's borders.

Each control on a report, each report section, and the report itself has a group of properties that you can work with on the property sheet to format that report

5

element. For a text box, you can set properties such as Width, Height, Back Color, Border Style, Border Color, Font Name, Font Size, and Text Align.

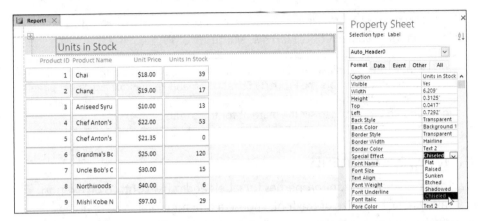

Setting the Special Effect property for a text box control.

For report sections (such as Detail, Page Header, and Page Footer), you can set the Height property to 0 inches to hide the section. For the Detail section, you can set the Can Grow and Can Shrink properties to Yes if you want the size of the Detail section to increase and decrease depending on the amount of information it displays for a specific record. The Report Header and Report Footer sections also have these properties.

For the Report Header and Report Footer sections and the Page Header and Page Footer sections, you can also set the Display When property to Always, Print Only, or Screen Only. If you add page numbers to the Page Footer section, for example, set the Display When property to Print Only to show the page numbers only when you print the report.

Report properties include the Default View property, which controls whether the report opens in Print preview or Report view by default. (The report opens in the view you specify for the Default View property when you right-click a report in the Navigation Pane and then click Open.)

To select controls on a report

→ On the report, select the control you want to format.

→ On the Format tool tab, in the **Selection** group, do either of the following:

- To select a specific control, expand the **Object** list, then click the control you want to format.

- To select all controls on the report, click **Select All**.

To format report controls

1. Open the report in Layout view and select the control or controls you want to format.

2. On the **Format** tool tab, in the **Font** group, choose a new font, font size, or font color; apply bold, italic, or underline formatting; add a background fill color; and align the text.

3. For number, currency, and date and time fields, use the commands in the **Number** group on the **Format** tool tab to apply number, date/time, and currency formatting to the field.

4. In the **Control Formatting** group on the **Format** tool tab, do the following:

   - Use the **Shape Fill** command to add a background fill color to a control.
   - Use the **Shape Outline** command to apply line styles and colors to the control's borders.

To set control and report properties

1. Open the report in Layout view and open the property sheet.

2. Select the control or report section you want to format.

3. In the property sheet, click in the box for the property you want to set, then select an option Access provides or enter the value you want to use.

Change report orientation

You can switch the report layout between portrait and landscape. *Portrait* prints across the shorter dimension of the paper, so it is best for reports that have only a few fields. *Landscape* prints across the long dimension of the paper, so use it if your report has many fields.

To specify page orientation for a report

1. Open the report in Layout view.

2. On the **Page Setup** tool tab, in the **Page Layout** group, click **Portrait** or **Landscape**.

5

Or

1. Open the report in Print Preview mode.

2. On the **Print Preview** tab, in the **Page Layout** group, click **Portrait** or **Landscape**.

Insert information in report headers and footers

In Layout view, you can use commands in the Header/Footer group of the Design tool tab to insert standard elements in a report's header and footer sections: a logo, a title, the date and time, and page numbers.

The Page Numbers command opens a dialog box in which you select a format, position, and alignment for page numbers. Page numbers appear in the Page Header or Page Footer section and can be centered or aligned at the left or right border. You can clear the check box for the Show Number On First Page option to start pagination on the report's second page.

Format and configure report page number with the Page Numbers dialog box.

To insert information in a report header or footer

1. Open the report in Layout view.

2. On the **Design** tool tab, in the **Header/Footer** group, do any of the following:

   - To add a logo to the report header, click **Logo**. In the **Insert Picture** dialog box, navigate to and select the logo image file, then click **Open**.

   - To add a title to the report header, click **Title**. In the **Auto_Header()** control that appears, replace the default title with the report title you want.

- To add the date or time to the report header, click **Date And Time**. In the **Date and Time** dialog box, select the check boxes for the elements you want to include, select the element formats you want, and then click **OK**.

- To add page numbers to the report header or footer, click **Page Numbers**. In the **Page Numbers** dialog box, click the format, position, and alignment you want. Then click **OK**.

Insert images on reports

Reports can display logos or images related to the purpose of the database—product thumbnails, project locations, or employee portraits, for example. You can also insert an image as the background for a report. Access offers quite a few properties that affect the appearance and behavior of the image.

See Also For a complete description of the properties that you can configure for an image, see "Insert images" in "Objective 4.2: Format forms."

To insert an image on a report

1. Open the report in Layout view.

2. On the **Design** tool tab, in the **Controls** group, click **Insert Image**, then do either of the following:

   - Select an image in the **Image** gallery.

   - Click **Browse** to locate the image file you want to use. Select the image file in the **Insert Picture** dialog box, then click **OK**.

3. Click the report at the position where you want the image to appear.

4. Open the report property sheet. At the top of the property sheet, in the **Selection Type** list, click the image name.

5. On the **Format** tab of the property sheet, set the values you want to use for the following properties: **Picture Type**, **Picture**, **Picture Tiling**, **Picture Alignment**, and **Picture Size Mode**.

5

To add an image to a report's background

1. Open the report in Layout view.

2. On the **Format** tool tab, in the **Background** group, click **Background Image**, then do either of the following:

   - Select an image in the **Image** gallery.
   - Click **Browse** to locate the image file you want to use. Select the image file in the **Insert Picture** dialog box, then click **OK**.

3. Open the report property sheet. At the top of the property sheet, in the **Selection Type** list, click **Report**.

4. On the **Format** tab of the property sheet, set the values you want to use for the following properties: **Picture Type**, **Picture**, **Picture Tiling**, **Picture Alignment**, and **Picture Size Mode**.

Objective 5.2 practice tasks

The practice file for these tasks is located in the **MOSAccessExpert2019\ Objective5** practice file folder. The folder also contains a result file that you can use to check your work.

➤ Open the **AccessExpert_5-2** database. If the Info Bar opens below the ribbon, click the *Enable Content* button.

➤ Open the Products report in Layout view and do the following:

❑ Set the control margins to *Wide* for all the controls.

❑ Adjust the height of all the controls to ***0.31 inches***.

❑ Add the date and time to the Header section of the form. In the report's property sheet, select the formats *Medium Date* and *Medium Time*, respectively.

❑ Change the report page orientation to Landscape.

❑ Set up a three-column report and set the column width to ***3 inches***.

❑ Arrange the fields to go down, and then across.

❑ Apply bold formatting to all the report labels.

❑ Select the Products Report label in the report header, apply bold and italic formatting, change the Font to Calibri Light, and set the font color to Dark Blue.

❑ For the Products Report label, set the Special Effect property to Shadowed.

❑ Display the report in print preview, then save and close the report.

➤ Open the **AccessExpert_5-2_results** database. Compare the two databases to check your work, then close the open databases.

Index

I

images, 124
  on forms, 135–136
  in reports, 155–156
Import Objects dialog box, 2–3
Import Spreadsheet Wizard, 41
Import Text Wizard, 42
importing
  data, 2–6, 40–41
    appending records, 47–49
    into new table, 41–47
  objects, 2–6
  queries, 3
  tables, 3, 52–54
inner joins, 21, 103
Input Mask Wizard, 81
input masks, 80–82
Insert Hyperlink dialog box, 119
inserting
  columns, 109
  fields, 74–77
    in queries, 109
  form controls, 118–120
  headers/footers
    in forms, 133–135
    in reports, 154–155
  images
    on forms, 135–136
    in reports, 155–156
  labels in reports, 145–146
  report controls, 143–145
  table descriptions, 60–61
  Total rows, 58–59

J

join lines, 21
joins
  in multiple–table queries, 102–104
  types of, 21
junction tables, 19–20

K

keys
  composite, 12
  foreign, setting, 17–18
  primary

  removing, 13
  setting, 12–13

L

labels, 123
  editing
    on forms, 126
    in reports, 145–146
  inserting in reports, 145–146
landscape orientation, 153
Layout view
  form controls
    headers/footers, 133–135
    images, 135–136
    inserting/removing, 118–120
    labels, 126
    margins/spacing, 132–133
    moving, 120–121
    setting properties, 122–126
    tab order, 129–131
  reports
    grouping/sorting records, 140–143
    headers/footers, 154–155
    images, 155–156
    inserting controls, 143–145
    labels, 145–146
    margins/spacing, 149–151
    multiple columns, 148–149
    orientation, 153–154
    properties, 151–153
layouts for forms, 121
left–outer joins, 21, 103
Linked Table Manager dialog box, 50
linked tables, creating, 49–52
linking tables, 19–20
List Box Wizard, 119
list boxes, 124
logical operators, 112

M

make-table queries
  creating, 100
  described, 98
many-to-many database model, 19–20
margins
  for form controls, 132–133
  for report controls, 149–151

Plug into learning at

MicrosoftPressStore.com

The Microsoft Press Store by Pearson offers:

- Free U.S. shipping

- Buy an eBook, get three formats – Includes PDF, EPUB, and MOBI to use with your computer, tablet, and mobile devices

- Print & eBook Best Value Packs

- eBook Deal of the Week – Save up to 50% on featured title

- Newsletter – Be the first to hear about new releases, announcements, special offers, and more

- Register your book – Find companion files, errata, and product updates, plus receive a special coupon* to save on your next purchase